LATTER REIGN

Latter Reign

Death Of A Seed To Life In A Promise

DENISE WEDINGTON JONES

Denise Wedington Jones

Latter Reign
Published by Denise Wedington Jones
Author website: www.authenticallynisei.com

Copyright © 2022 by Denise Wedington Jones
All rights reserved.

ISBN 978-0-578-29974-7 (softcover)
ISBN 978-0-578-2995-4 (ebook)

Requests for information should be addressed to:
1441 Halyard Way SE Townsend, GA 31331

All Scripture quotations, unless otherwise indicated, are taken from THE MESSAGE. Copyright © 1993, 2002, 2018 by Eugene H. Peterson. Used by permission of NavPress. All rights reserved. Represented by Tyndale House Publishers, Inc.
Scripture quotations marked (AMP) are taken from the Amplified Bible, Copyright © 1954, 1958, 1962, 1964, 1965, 1987 by The Lockman Foundation. Used by permission.
Scripture quotations marked KJ21 are taken from the 21st Century King James Version®, copyright © 1994. Used by permission of Deuel Enterprises, Inc., Gary, SD 57237. All rights reserved.

Scripture quotations marked KJV are taken from the King James Version, public domain.

Scripture quotations marked TLB are from The Living Bible, copyright © 1971 by Tyndale House Foundation. Used by permission of Tyndale House Publishers Inc., Carol Stream, Illinois 60188. All rights reserved. The Living Bible, TLB, and the The Living Bible logo are registered trademarks of Tyndale House Publishers.

Any internet addresses (websites, blogs, etc.) and telephone numbers in this book are offered as a resource. They are not intended in any way to be or imply an endorsement by Denise Wedington Jones, nor does Denise Wedington Jones vouch for the content of these sites and numbers for the life of this book.

No part of this publication may be reproduced, stored in a retrieval system, or transmitted in any form or by any means—electronic, mechanical, photocopy, recording, or any other—except for brief quotations in printed reviews, without the prior permission of the publisher.

Cover illustration and design: Denise Wedington Jones
Interior design: Denise Wedington Jones

Printed in the United States of America

*This book is dedicated to First and always first -
God. I love you, and this story is Yours.
Get the glory.*

To my mom, JoAnn. Mom, I did it! I know you would be proud to know that I finished this work. Thank you for your love and support. Thank you for constantly reminding me God has so much more for me. Thank you for being my mom. Rest in His Love.

To my husband James, and my children ZaTascha Cy'mone and Curtis Lavon (CJ). Your faith in me is unparalleled. You pushed me when I didn't want to be pushed and believed in me when I didn't believe in myself. Thank you.

To my best friend Kimberly, girl, you have been there from day one! Thank you for being my sister and very best friend. I love you.

*To my sister Ruth. You inspire me.
I always said I want to be like you when I grow up.
I think I may be getting there! Love you.*

CONTENTS

DEDICATION - v
FOREWARD - ix
INTRODUCTION - x

~ 1 ~
The Beginning of the End
1

~ 2 ~
The Trauma of It All
21

~ 3 ~
The Caved Bird Set Free
32

~ 4 ~
Marriage Matters – A Poem
37

~ 5 ~
The Cross I Made
44

~ 6 ~
Stupid Is as Stupid Does
60

~ 7 ~

Waiting to Begin...Again

72

~ 8 ~

It's Never Too Late

94

~ 9 ~

It Only Takes Faith

98

~ 10 ~

The Reigning Season

109

ABOUT THE AUTHOR - 115

FOREWORD

Sometimes life can seem calm and smooth, but then for some reason unknown to most of us, life can be a total disruption. It can be hard, with no end to the pain in sight.

God entrusted Denise Wedington-Jones with a hard life because He knew that He could depend on her to come through as a champion. As you read the pages of this book you will feel a myriad of emotions---sadness, anger, disbelief, and finally joy. She made it—never would have made it without God. But she has lived through it and gives God all the honor, glory, and praise. He stood by her and enabled her to sustain life, that she might help others find their way to light in this world.

Her story is not a fairy tale. It is not a feel-good Hallmark story. It is a hard-to-imagine, hard-to-read reminder that whatever you are going through, someone else may be going through worse. It is a full circle reminder that God said He will never leave us nor forsake us, and wherever we are, He's there, even in the most hellish situation.

This is a story of hope, triumph, and the power of faith in a loving God who does not always move our mountains but gives us the strength to climb them.

God is doing great things with this author. This is not the end, so jump in and begin this journey with her and see what God will do next.

Janice Rhodes Casey
Minister and Author
Founder of *God's Toolbox* Podcast

INTRODUCTION

~ written from the tables of my heart

The moment it was spoken to my heart concerning writing a book about my life, I knew the struggle would be real. I was attending a women's conference at a church, and the woman of God – a prophetess – came to me and spoke to me so clearly saying, " *God said you are going to write three books and they shall be successful."* I thought she was crazy! *Me? Write a book?* I could not fathom writing a book at that time because I was in the midst of a great spiritual battle. All I wanted from the Lord was a word of comfort that everything would be okay. God did send me a word, but it was not what I expected nor what I thought I wanted. God shows the prophet a vision of what is or what will be. The prophet then proclaims the vision to the person or to a people. It was the prophet's job to tell me what God showed her, and it was my job to respond to it. Little did I know that the prophecy spoken to me was already taking place through my experiences.

I used to love to write before *life* started happening, so it was a feasible thought but one I had not perceived in a long time. I had written a book of poems and an article series about purpose in a Christian magazine yet could not fathom that God had desired more for me.

The beginning of a dream or desire coming to pass takes several stages for one to go through, and I was in one of those stages but didn't realize it until later on. My life was in utter turmoil and I had no idea that I was experiencing stages of the prophetic word spoken because it was so very painful. It felt like I would never get to the end of pain. I felt as though God was nowhere to be found at that time, although the Word of God says he will never leave us nor forsake us. It took every ounce of my being to not look at her and say something back to hurt her like I was hurting. I didn't say a word. I simply smiled and raised my hands to receive the word of the prophetess, and after she prayed for me, I sat down outwardly quiet, while my heart was inwardly screaming.

It wasn't her fault, and she didn't know I was going through anything really. I wore the perfect church face. My mother taught us to never allow anyone to see you looking bad when you felt your worst. So, I would dress my very best and go on through the day as if the world was bright and sunny, when in reality, my heart was drowning in the flood of tears that soaked my pillow every night. Going through trials without others is lonely, but I could not trust myself to let anyone in – especially those I went to church with because they were the ones who looked upon my trial as though I was sinning if I voiced my pain. I couldn't tell anyone but God and maybe one or two friends who I knew would understand. I was doing all I knew to do to maintain myself and not give *"my testimony before coming through the test."* The Bible speaks of going through trials of fire and how to go through them successfully, but no one prepares you for the type of heat that comes along with the fire.

I felt as though I was dying - and I was. I was dying to the life I thought I should have had. I was dying to all the pain that I suffered without an explanation. I was dying to my own thoughts and inclinations of what my life and my family's lives should be like. God was giving me a new heart and a renewed mind. Every hard place, every wrong turn, every bad relationship was for a reason. God saved me, built my faith in him, and walked with me through every situation in my life. He set me on a path and journey I didn't know of and walked with me in the wilderness where I never thought I'd survive. He brought me to an oasis of his love and trusted me with my trials in order to share my story with you.

I remember telling a small part of what I was going through at a women's meeting, and afterwards being pulled into the pastor's office to be reprimanded about it. I was disillusioned because I thought I could share amongst women who should have understood, but instead I was told that what I said was not a testimony. Every opportunity to say something afterwards was stifled by that reprimand in my mind. I decided that if I was going to get through this, I had to rely on God alone and that is what I did. In the church of the Lord, the Ecclesia, you should be able to get the love and understanding from those who you surround yourself with in ministry, but sadly sometimes, you cannot. We enter into salvation as broken vessels needing to be restored. It takes real spiritual and personal maturity in Christ to become the type of person who simply loves and does not and will not judge you according to the flesh. Sadly, the church can look upon you in judgment and sometimes disdain. I couldn't tell my sister or mother, because they had their own trials they were going through. Although they knew some of my struggles, they did not know it all, and I purposed in my heart that if God was with me, then he would see me through. I have made so many mistakes - or lessons - as I call them - and learned from them all.

This book contains a part of my journey, the lessons I learned, and the hope that Christ brings as you walk through life's difficulties. Some of the stories here are raw, but I made a promise to the Lord that I would write as the Holy Spirit led me to write, and he wanted this written in its transparency, and every story is my truth as I experienced it. For so many years, I did not believe my story had value or carried importance. Every time I felt the nudging of the Holy Spirit to begin to write this book, I struggled, because I felt this book would be for nothing. Then I learned that every great writer has struggled over their best work, and I became encouraged; but still I could not write. I let years go by and would try to hide this truth from rising in my heart by filling up my time.

I returned to college at the age of forty-something and not only received my Bachelor of Science in Psychology degree but Master of Science degree in Counseling and Life Coaching, and a Master of Science degree in Psychology and Health. I began to mentor others and coach women as part of my career and kept very busy. It was at this time in my life when I recognized God calling me to help women through their trials by sharing parts of my life with them. As I walked alongside them in whatever they seemed to face. I was encouraged and I gained a renewed sense of purpose. Prior to getting my degrees and coaching women, I worked in the church at whatever I could find to do. I loved the children's ministry and worked there for many years. I was also a part of the worship team and other parts of the ministry simply helping because my heart was called to do it and I wanted to be a blessing.

I worked so much I experienced burn-out. I was still going through my own personal struggles and wanted to serve my pastor and the ministry I knew I was called to. But I felt God leading me to come to Himself, and that was very difficult for me. I relied so much on others, that I had not realized that I was not listening to God as much as I was listening to people. He wanted me to hear him, so I withdrew to be alone and he taught me how to pray.

The more I prayed and sought the Lord, the more I felt the nudge to go on this journey with Him alone. I didn't know what to do because I was told that I was called to the ministry, but God was calling me too. One day, he spoke this to my heart, *You are doing good works, but not God works, and this is what I am calling you to.* I was floored and I cried for many days and nights because I knew that it would cause a separation from those whom I loved and served. Sometimes, you will be separated from those who you depend upon and love. Sometimes, the separation will be permanent, and at other times the separation is for a season. If He is calling you to come away with him, you have to go. It will be for the good, and always for His glory.

After leaving the ministry and going alone with the Lord, I began to really learn about myself. There was nothing to fill up my time but Him, and I had to listen. He has taken me on a walk of faith unlike anything I have ever experienced. It's one thing to look to people for answers, but when the Lord encloses you into himself, your eyes can see only one way and that is up! I was a moth. A caterpillar of God's personal tutor the Holy Spirit. He wrapped me in his love and in his teachings in the Scripture, and I learned truly that Christ is all in all. He is in all of my good, and in all of my bad. He took my life as I knew it and turned it right-side up. He placed His laws in my heart and in my mind, and I began to live and walk it out in a sense of freedom I had not had before. He showed me that I had to die to my ways so that I can live in him. Then his dreams for my life can be fulfilled. He taught me faith and he taught me the only way to gain in this new kingdom life is to lose my old natural one.

What do you do when you walk with God in seasons of aloneness? Where is God when it feels like he is nowhere to be found? How did I find myself in situations I never thought I would ever be a part of? Where is a good God in all the things? In this book, I take you on my journey. The good, some of the bad and the ugly, so you can see that Christ our Redeemer lives. He can take your life and make you brand new. He can bring you from victimization to victory. From being overwhelmed to overcoming. He can reshape your mind and give you wisdom and bring your real life – the life in him forward. He can make your past mistakes, your present stepping stones towards a future and a hope!

It is my hope that as you read it, you feel what I went through, take something from it, and perhaps share what you learn about me with others. Perhaps this story written from the tables of my heart can help you gain the courage you need to write your own story and pave the way God has set for your life without shame. Be victorious in your authenticity. Be yourself in your truth, as you walk out your journey in transparency before God.

~ 1 ~

THE BEGINNING OF THE END

"A journey of a thousand miles begins with a single step" - Lao Tzu

"Put one foot in front of the other..." came from a song from a childhood Christmas movie that I loved to watch. It spoke of overcoming fear and going forward. I thought as I grew up as an adult that I would be going forward and become successful in life. Little did I know that I had a long way to go for that. I wanted to change, but I have not yet become the woman I was designed and purposed to be. Why? Inside I was still the little girl whose view of life was tainted from perverse paintings of what men were to me. I was a little princess looking for her king, the man who was supposed to be there to take care of me.

He died, my dad, and in the stench of his death my freedom flitted away as a feather in the wind drifting listlessly wherever the wind would carry it. I stood in my blue dress with pleated skirting and a sheer jacket with white piping staring at everyone at the funeral. I was five. It was weird to see everyone dressed in black but me. My mother had a lace veil over her face which could not cover the streams of tears which streamed so violently down, dripping faucet-like in a pool on her lap. My aunt was sitting behind us, and I could hear her faint whimpering turning into a full-blown wail. I didn't know it then, but my family was so emotionally charged...so filled with drama, it would be unable to teach me, to rear me, and to mold and shape me into the image of who I am.

Someone came up behind me and lifted me high into the air to see what was in the shiny box with flowers around it. As I was lifted, I could smell every lily and carnation. The striking smell deafening me. I peered into the box and looked inside at the man that was lying there. He looked like my dad, but different. The face was clay-like and stiff-looking. There was no elasticity, there was no softness like the face I knew - like the cheek I rubbed when he carried me. It was my dad alright, but it wasn't because he wouldn't wake up. Whomever was holding me gently leaned me in so I could kiss him, and I did. He was cold. As I was being brought back up, I saw these things behind his earlobes. I didn't know it at the time, but they were clamps holding his skin taut and in place.

They lowered me down and I sat back down next to my siblings and watched my mother go to the box to do what I did, look at the clay man who was now my dad. She could barely stand. I know she couldn't see through her tears, but there she was - my mother. My strong but sad mother breaking apart in front of me. I wanted to go to her, but there were so many people surrounding her. So, I put my head down and I said a prayer and asked God to help us. That day was so hard for everyone. My mom was sad, my siblings were sad, my granddad was sad. He was so sad, that he didn't live too many more years after my dad. Our family suffered so much loss in so little time, Yet this was just the beginning.

Blessed, Broken, and Purposed

Oprah Winfrey said, *"I've come to believe that each of us has a personal calling that's as unique as a fingerprint - and that the best way to succeed is to discover what you love and then find a way to offer it to others in the form of service, working hard, and also allowing the energy of the universe to lead you."* This uniqueness was something I didn't know I had within me. I was so young. I was a baby when my dad died. I was five years old and could barely spell my name let alone understand purpose. But God still had a divine purpose for my life. In the Bible, God spoke to Jeremiah as a youth and said: *"Before I shaped you in the womb, I knew all about you. Before you saw the light of day, I had holy plans for you: A prophet to the nations* (Jeremiah 1:5 MSG)

Jeremiah, like all of us, was born for a specific purpose in the plan of God - to glorify Him in the earth. He gave the very first chosen people a mandate. According to scripture:

> *God created human beings.*
> *He created them godlike,*
> *Reflecting God's nature.*
> *He created them male and female.*
> *God blessed them:*
> *"Prosper! Reproduce! Fill Earth! Take charge!*
> *Be responsible for fish in the sea and birds in the air,*
> *for every living thing that moves on the face of Earth.*
> *(Genesis 1: 27 - 28 MSG)*

What a blessing to know that we are created for a specific purpose to honor our Creator with our whole selves as *He* in turn blesses our lives in the earth! My unique fingerprint was in me since birth. I felt as a small child that I was different, and my mom knew as well. I had a connection with my Creator very early, and I knew that. How did I know? I would pray every day. I learned to pray from attending church with my mom.

The pastor would call for people to kneel at their seats or come to the front of the church to the altar to pray. My mom would then tell us to kneel at our seats. I took that as a very serious time. In the church my family joined you did not play around when it was time to pray. We attended a small store front church in the heart of the city I lived in. Our pastors were husband and wife. The wife was head pastor and her husband co-pastored with her. This woman was beautiful and powerful in the Spirit. She spoke with such confidence and strength, and I could tell my mother really loved being there with the other members.

In this church, there were ushers who wore white nursing dresses with white stockings and white nurse's shoes. They even wore nursing caps. These ladies were definitely to be feared and they directed everyone during our Sunday service. They were like soldiers and they were formidable. If they pointed a finger at you, you knew you were in trouble. If you were called to the back to sit with one of them, you were in for a stern talking to. These women had a purpose and it was to maintain the holiness and order of the house of God. Early in my childhood I learned about order and decency in the church. The church has purpose; it is a place of instruction and structure, and a holy place where we come to honor and worship God and hear the preached Word of God. I was taught early how to conduct myself in the church, and I did so obediently.

At the time of prayer, children were told to kneel and be quiet. I would listen as others prayed and I would start to talk to Jesus too. I would ask him to bless my mom and to bless my family. I had the child-like faith in him that the Scriptures speak of. This was the beginning of learning about Jesus.

My mother prayed all the time, and so did my grandmother. Those two women were my examples of powerful praying. I would watch the tears stream down my grandmother's cheeks as she prayed, and I loved to watch them praise the Lord. Back then we called it 'catching the Holy Ghost.' I'm not sure who coined that phrase but we all knew what it meant. When someone 'caught the Holy Ghost' that person would gyrate and move in a rhythm which caused onlookers to know they were experiencing God. My grandmother's way of 'catching the Holy Ghost' was shaking and jerking, and loudly praising God. It was scary and funny at the same time. As a child I did not know what she was really doing, but I knew instinctively she was getting her prayers to God.

There were other times too when the children would have to be removed from the sanctuary because someone needed special prayer. This moment was when I realized that satan and demons are real. I witnessed a woman who was receiving prayer for being possessed by a devil. Some of you may not believe that there are spiritual realms with angels and devils, but it is very real. There is much skepticism about this subject, however, the holy Scriptures clearly prove that demons and angelic beings are real, and they are active in our earth realm and realms in the heavens. Dr. Marta Illueca in her work at Yale Divinity School wrote, although she had no intention on proving or disproving the existence of spirits, those with spiritual afflictions should seek out pastoral care for deliverance ministry. This ministry includes but is not limited to specific prayer for deliverance, and a team of ministers, social service agents, and psychologists.

In the past, people were brought to the church for spirits to be cast out. The Scriptures clearly speak of instances where people who were possessed by demonic spirits were brought to Jesus and He cast the devils out of them. The apostles in the New Testament also had power to do the same. In Matthew 10 verse 8 Jesus said every believer will have the power to "Heal the sick, cleanse the lepers, raise the dead, cast out devils: freely ye have received, freely give." Every born again person has been given power in Christ to accomplish great things in the earth, but many do not really believe in the supernatural power of God. I knew that God was great, and there was and is something great He has given me. I also knew the devil was real; I just didn't know how he operated, and I certainly didn't know that he is an enemy who would try to crush my purpose even before I began.

There was something very different about how I viewed the world around me. I would have dreams and they would happen. I would just 'know' things before they occurred. People call it Deja Vue. I did not know it was the gift of my calling from God. I just allowed things to be. It was very natural to me. Although I did not know exactly what I was seeing, I knew that God was showing me. How you ask? It was a knowing – a voice on the inside of my heart telling me that what I saw was the truth. I believed that God was speaking to me. I had peace and calm inside when I heard his voice and I knew that I was safe, even at times when I felt afraid. It had to be God showing me things before they happened. No one else has that type of power.

I was a child, but I also trusted what my mother and grandmother taught us about Jesus. I believed what I felt in my heart and the visions I saw, and he proved it to me by those things coming to pass. In the book of 1 Samuel chapter 9 verse 9 it reads, *"In former times in Israel, a person who wanted to seek God's word on a matter would say, "Let's visit the Seer," because the one we now call "the Prophet" was also called "the Seer."* I didn't know that I was a prophetic person. I just knew I saw things.

My grandmother was a seer as well. She was born with a "veil" over her face. What this means is she was born with a birth caul or a membrane of the amniotic sac covering her. It covers the face like a cloth and is removed at birth. In Black folklore, it often meant that the child born with a veil had the ability to see the supernatural and to know the future. She was prophetic, and so am I. I was not born with a veil, but I was born on a full moon. My dad's grandmother predicted my birth by the moon and as she said it, I was born on that day. I am blessed to see in the realm of the spirit. Because of this gift, I was also a target for the enemy, the devil who seeks to destroy my life.

The seer or prophet is called a *nabiy'* according to Hebrew text. It is a person who speaks on behalf of God. God uses prophets to give instruction and direction to his people. Every prophet is different and the administration of the prophet's office is unique to God's design of that individual, yet the overarching message is the same. We are called to testify of Christ. I am called as a watchman and I am called as God's messenger in the earth. I see and give insight. I foresee and give foresight. I forth see and give forth sight. I am made for the pleasure of God and am a horn in His mouth according to 1 Chronicles 25:5. I am called to testify of the Lord Jesus *for the testimony of Jesus is the spirit of prophecy* – Revelation 19:10.

As a prophetic child, it was difficult to understand why I suffered at the hands of people who I thought would love and care for me, but it was the enemy who used those closest to me to harm me. It was very scary to experience some of the difficulties I went through, and for many years could not understand the 'why' behind it. Even after understanding who I am in Christ, it took a long time before the pieces came together for me.

Popular evangelist and speaker Joyce Meyer once said that hurt people hurt others, and this is very true. At three years of age, I did not know that those who hurt me were also hurting and broken as they tried and succeeded in breaking me. I didn't know the things I was about to suffer was due to satan, his devices and sin in this world. I only knew I felt unprotected and alone. My dad had a friend or a running buddy. He would be with my dad when my dad went to play pool at the pool hall. Purcell (that was his name) was always around. He was a person I didn't like at all. He would hold me in a way that was so uncomfortable. I didn't like being in the back seat of the car with him. We didn't have car seats, so I had to sit near him or on his lap. I hated being near him. He gave me the creeps, but I couldn't say anything to my dad. I stayed silent. I wanted to be what I thought was a good girl. This was the beginning of the assault on my life that took me spiraling down a pathway of disaster.

My life became worse shortly after my dad died. My life had not begun, yet the path before me was difficult, and I was too young to understand, let alone to navigate the way I should have taken. I had a soft heart, was very trusting, and easily led into things, but I also knew that I was fiercely loyal to and protective of my mother. Although my mom could not protect me fully from the deceit of the devil and those he used to bring harm in my life, God had a plan. He knew what he planted in my heart before I was born, and he was going to ensure that it would come to fruition. Until then, I journeyed along a route laid out to destroy me, and I would discover who was really on my side. This began with my parents.

The Groundbreaking – Their Broken Lives & My Shattered Pieces

My parents met as teenagers. My mom and dad lived in the same housing project and they began dating. My mother became pregnant at the age of 14 and had my oldest sister. It was a very tumultuous relationship because they were too young to date and in the 1960's it was shameful for a young girl to become pregnant so young. I do not have all the details behind their life in the early stages, but they remained together. My mom married my dad and they had five children before she turned 22.

Dad was drafted into the Army during the Vietnam War three days after I was born, and while there he was injured. During this horrific war, Black people were under-represented, and were highest in number assigned to combat zones. There were some military bases who paraded around in Ku Klux Klan hoods and it was not uncommon to see crosses burning on bases in this aggressive country. It was very difficult for Black men in the military in the 1960's and 70's. Racism was rampant in the war zones where they battled and in the base camps where they lived for so many months away from home. After the death of Martin Luther King Jr., Black troops still could not be proud to serve their country in a foreign place. Although racial segregation was banned, it remained amongst some of the troops in the war.

For my dad and many soldiers like him who fought during this time, the issues of racist fighting was not lost on those who served a country which denied them their basic rights as people of color. In those years dad served in an army which did not recognize his merit because of the color of his skin, and he became broken. He was broken from being drafted into a war he didn't start. He was broken from the harm, degradation, and pain from his fellow countrymen, and he was broken from the wounds of his time serving our country.

My dad was injured while fighting in Vietnam. He stepped on a land mine while saving his partner and lost the lower half of his left leg. He received the Purple Heart which was awarded to those who were wounded or killed as a result of enemy action. It is a medal of distinction and means that a servicemember paid a high price and sacrificed himself in the line of duty. My dad definitely paid a very high price. He came home broken in mind, body, and soul. The injury required medication, and dad was given an opiate drug called morphine to ease his pain. He became hooked on that drug and became an addict. After he returned home, my dad was not the same person he was prior to the war.

He was different. The Vietnam war ravaged him and left him broken into pieces. My mom had to go through so much with him. From police raids for drugs in our home to walking my dad when he overdosed to keep him alive. We watched our lives completely shatter before us. He was murdered a few weeks before Christmas. Someone left him in the back seat of our car with nothing on his body but his underwear. That year Christmas was not a happy time. He was robbed, and on that day, so were we.

We believed my dad's injury ultimately cost him his life, and the life he wanted for his family. What purpose did my dad's life and death serve? I know that without him, I would not have been born. I'm glad he was my dad, and I miss the opportunity to have him in my life. I loved my dad. I wanted him to be around and raise us. I was five when he passed away in 1971, but I remember him as if it were yesterday. His death broke us! Literally!

My mom was left behind with five children to raise all on her own. We lived in project housing, but my mom became this warrior after dad's death. We weren't poor by our standards. Mom always drove a new car, and she made our apartment into a home. She taught us the value of having things and to appreciate what we had.

As I look back, I see how hard my mom really worked to provide for us. She had her faults, after all she was human, but even in her faults her heart was to make sure her kids were cared for. My mom dedicated her life to not only her children, but she also reached out to help other kids, and raised children who were not hers biologically. She worked herself to the bone and when she injured her lower spine in a fall, she still tried to work and make sure everyone was ok.

The Great Inflation caused everyone to take a dive financially, and my family suffered. In the years of inflation in the 1970's and 1980's there were lines for food, gas, and little to no employment opportunities. We had to have food stamps back then. The food assistance was not like it is today. We had what was called books of stamps. We would take our grocery cart and walk to Pantry Pride, the only supermarket in our neighborhood, to shop for food. We would tear the stamps which were made like the denominations of money, to pay for our food. Sometimes, mom would get stamps from other family members but the serial numbers didn't match the book, so she would tell us to stick them in there and pretend when we was paying for food that we were tearing the stamps from that particular book. It is funny now that I remember back as I would make a grand show of tearing the stamps from the book, knowing that it was not the right one. Being on food stamps and getting in long lines for the surplus food items the government gave out to the poor was sad and shameful, but we loved the cheese we received. We called it 'government cheese'. We could make a great grilled cheese sandwich from that cheese. It was thick and so creamy when melted in the frying pan. I loved those sandwiches!

I know mom felt really bad and I know that she continued to provide for us as best she could. As we matured and were old enough to work, each one of us obtained jobs to help out my mom. I didn't want her to have to pay for our clothes, so I worked to get the things I wanted. I wanted to remove some of the burden from her shoulders.

We were a low income, single-parent family for many years. My mom was broken by her life's circumstances, we were broken by the death of our dad, and in that brokenness, the shattering of my young life began. The ground of my heart contained the sadness of my life and it began when I became abused. What do you do, when your mom is brokenhearted, trying to raise her children, and in the midst of this, there are predators lurking around her home? Let me give you a typical day in the house:

Uncovering the Mess

"Clean up this house!" My mother yelled at us as she walked in from work. My sister, oldest brother and I were in the kitchen and they were arguing at whose turn it was to wash the dishes. We lived in a housing project called Brook Sloate. I, as the middle child of five, who according to author Brandon Specktor, is the neglected one, was the team player, the best friend maker, the humble little bumble bee in the sea of other bees. Middle children are supposed to be leaders, great lovers (well that is true) and people who thrive…not merely survive! *Really?* Well, I could not see that at the time. I saw other things as a small child that pushed me into a corner and made me cringe away from attention, even though I secretly craved love. I digress. Back to my siblings and mom.

My mom gave us chores that we had to complete weekly. Someone had dishes and the kitchen, someone else cleaned both bathrooms. I hated when it was my week to do the bathrooms because I had brothers. They can be so dirty when they are small boys. Someone else had to wash all the clothes and hang them on the "line" outside to dry. Then we had to bring them in, fold them, separate the ironing clothes, then iron all of those and hang them up. Another had to vacuum and sweep all the rooms. My mom had a well-oiled machine in the house with us and the chores, the apartment was *always* clean.

After my dad died, a few years had passed and we settled into a routine. We moved from one housing project to another and my mom put us into school and continued working as a nurse's assistant for the hospitals and nursing homes in the city. As a single mother with five children, my mom worked very hard to give us the best she could. She was my hero. I worshipped the ground she walked on and nothing, I mean *nothing* she did was wrong. I wanted my mother to see me as a good girl. I never wanted to disappoint her, and I never, ever wanted to make her angry. She made me feel like I owed her that.

I don't think it was her intention, but as I got older, it seemed what I thought about came true. I don't mean that in a bad way; she was alone raising all of us, and she had very high expectations for each of her children. She expected us to excel in school and grow up to excel in life, and there's no wrong in expecting that. Mom worked hard, she played hard, and she lived her life her way. She was a survivor raising us to thrive in a cement playground with no soft landing. She was one tough cookie, but I know where she got her mental toughness from: it came from Grammy, our mom's mother. There's so much I can say about the matriarch of our family and I will, but for now, I want to talk about when my family and my broken pieces became shattered.

We were a typical very low-income Black family of the '70s, living in New Jersey, in poverty with my mom breaking her back to care for us and to provide clothing, shoes, food, shelter, transportation – you know, the necessities of life. We all lived near one another: my aunt lived in Fifth Avenue Projects, my uncles and their wives lived in The Terrace and Christopher Columbus Projects (CCP) respectively. We used to live in CCP, but "we moved on up to the East side and to de-luxe apartments in the skyyyy". Oops, I got lost for a moment in the song from a show called *The Jeffersons*. Maybe some of you know it, a hilarious show about a family who owned a cleaning business after moving from the projects to an apartment was similar to *Good Times* about people living in poverty in the projects. Funny how we all sat and watched those shows every day – even though we were already living that life. We could relate to these shows because we saw the same scenarios every day in our own community.

The negative connotations subconsciously reached us. I see now in retrospect how that show kept us living in poverty. It never had a storyline that gave us hope. Even when George and Louise (Weezy), his wife, moved into a nicer apartment and had a maid, it did not give us hope that one day we would be that way. It was fantasy - mere fantasy and had a sort of Uncle Tom tone to it.

Now don't get me wrong, I sat faithfully in front of the television to watch that and other shows like it...but what did it bring to produce fruitfulness in my life? Even when the Jeffersons moved next door to the Bunkers - Edith and bigoted Archie, all the show did was placed a black family in another impossible situation. What was wrong with this picture? Everything, but that was what American TV networks were selling to Blacks. Years later in the '80s the Cosby show came to television which depicted a black man who was a doctor married to a successful lawyer who raised their family in a beautiful Brooklyn brownstone. It did show us that black people can be successful and have a good life; but again...for those like me who came from an impoverished place with no guidance as to how to attain that life, it seemed like a dream. An impossible dream.

Death and Dreams

There is death that came with impoverished living. Dysfunction in families robs them of a rich, full life. It steals away joy, peace, love, and respect for one another. It can make the family turn on one another and become animalistic, yet when someone outside of the family intrudes, we come together like a pack to devour. It was a sick unity.

The Bible teaches Jesus came that we have an abundant life, but we did not know that – yet. We were religious like most blacks we knew. As a young girl I tagged along with my mom as we went to church and *"praised the Lawd"*, but there was no life...only death.

Every week on Sunday, we got up early in the morning and put on our best dresses and the boys their best pants and shirts. My mom would stand at the bottom of the stairs and yell, "Let's go!" and we'd hustle down the stairs and pile into the car. We went to several churches in my childhood. The one I remember most was a small store front church called Faith Soul Saving Station.

It was there I received my first baptism and my first real embarrassment. That small church had only one aisle, and you had to go up that aisle to use the bathroom. This particular Sunday, I went to the restroom, and when I came out, the ushers couldn't catch me in time, and there I pranced back to my seat with my dress stuck in my underwear in the back! Every kid laughed and the adults just shook their heads. I was mortified! One nice lady pulled me to her and snatched my dress down and sent me on my way to the front of the church where my mom sat. I was so ashamed. Why didn't the ushers stop me? Those ushers didn't play with you. They also took the noisy children out and scared Jesus into them so they would behave when they came back into the service. I was really afraid of them. As a child, I used to be very fearful. I was afraid for myself and for my family. I was scared most of the time until I prayed. It was lots of prayer going up then, but our family was still suffering. We suffered from lack of knowledge and fear. Fear can grip families and cause them to stay stuck. I was a scary child. I think it came from watching scary movies late at night when I couldn't sleep, and from my uncles scaring us by hiding walkie-talkies in closets when we were at my grandmother's house for the weekend. It was nothing for those teenagers to scare the little ones as they would often do to my younger brothers and me. I would hide from them as much as I could whenever we had to stay at my grandmother's. Hiding became natural for me. I know hiding made me feel safe, but there was another place where I felt safe.

If I could find any safety at all, it was when I was with my grandmother. She was my mom's mother. I called her *Grammy*.

I remember the time when my parents were physically fighting and my grandmother came to the rescue. I asked her what happened to her forehead. She had an old scar there. She very easily told me that she was hit in the face with a glass gallon milk jug by my step grandfather. I could imagine how badly that hurt her. Those glass milk bottles which were delivered to our doorstep every week were made of thick glass. They were very heavy. I imagined if someone swung that bottle to hit someone with it, that person would have more than a concussion! That showed me that my grandmother was a strong woman.

My Grammy was something to behold. She was beautiful, bold with big legs and wide hips. She wore her dresses with dignity and a swing to her gait filled with confidence. She was quietly bold. She knew things before anyone else did. God showed her things and revealed things to her that others didn't have the privilege to know.

Grammy could see things others could not. When she dreamt of fish, someone was always pregnant. She just had a "knowing" about her. Her aura was mysterious, but there was something else too. There seemed to be a deep sadness within her. I couldn't tell if she knew it was there, but I saw it. If she knew something, she would keep it to herself, but would hint around at what she knew; yet there were those times when she would not say what needed to be said. She was a fighter. She was forced to. She fought my step-granddad because he was abusive. She worked hard too but was a detached mother and not very affectionate: So was my mom. I guess that is why I thought Grammy was my safety. She and my mom were so much alike, and at times they did not get along. Mom and Grammy would have arguments.

Grammy was amazing, but like every human being, Grammy had flaws. Still, she was held in such high regard by those around her. She would babysit all of us at her home when mom had to work. We would play in the yard and run around her house on East 25th Street and would be so free! She wasn't living in housing and it made me feel like one day I could be just like her.

Grammy worked in the same field of nursing as my mom. She took care of the elderly in their homes and in Nursing facilities for long term care. Grammy had friends, but not too many. She had a quiet strength and she loved quietly as well. She wasn't a live out loud kind of woman, but her example spoke volumes. We would have cook-outs at Grammy's house and it would be so much fun for all of us. We also had picnics at a place called Garrett Mountain on holidays like July fourth. Those times made me know my family was close and they loved one another.

But then there were those times, when fighting would happen and those days would disappear from memory as fast as they entered. My mother and dad fought one another at the weirdest times. It would be at night, or after we had a family gathering. I never understood what triggered either one of them but seeing them fight was scary.

When my dad was killed, I'm not sure if Grammy saw that too – but I did in my dreams. When the police came to the house to tell my mother my dad was dead, I was in the living room. I felt that something was wrong, but I was a child. After they told my mom and she left with them to identify dad's body, I stared out of the window and my dream replayed in my mind.

This confirmed to me I was different, but still poverty and struggle changes you. It makes you become more than you may want, and not enough of what you need. Our poverty broke us – literally. Yet in the midst of the broken lives and all the mess that accompanies it, there was light in our family tunnel. God had something in store for this family. He had something in store for me. I only needed to take that first step to begin again on a new path enlightened by the force which has always driven me and guided me. Oprah calls it a unique fingerprint led by the energy of the Universe, is a poignant way to describe my specialness as a human being and God divinely saying *Yes! I matter.*

Life Lesson 1: - You Matter!

I love rainbows! The beauty of a rainbow after the rain or even in the midst of a cloudy sky simply brightens my day and reminds me there is a promise ahead. The story of Noah in the scriptures is where I draw hope that although bad things happen, there is light at the end. God told Noah that He was going to destroy everything he made due to the wickedness of men. He gave Noah instructions to build a vessel and told him exactly what to let in his vessel to be saved. Only Noah, his family, and those things which God commanded him to gather into the ark was saved as God wiped the earth clean.

In the times when Noah had to trust God and build that vessel, he kept his heart pure before the Lord and God counted him and his family worthy to restore the earth and its people with the living things set aside in the ark. When God caused the flood and wiped the earth clean from wickedness, He gave to Noah a great blessing: one, Noah and his family were kept alive. Two, all the things Noah brought into the ark was to be used to replenish the earth. Three, God had a plan and he was using one family to be a huge part of it. Can you imagine? Stepping out of that ark and being the only family on the entire earth!

The earth wasn't new, but God used Noah and the fact that he stood for goodness to bring people into the earth through his seed. Noah and his family mattered – and so do you! Whatever has happened in your life which did not seem so good, know that God can bring good out of it. Being born is not a burden, it is a blessing. What we do here on earth matters because God has a purpose for everything here. You may not see it right at this moment, but if you will look closer, lean into your life a bit more, you can see that there is a rainbow in your future. All things have purpose, even when it looks bad. Wiping the earth clean to start again was God's way of bringing something good out of bad. What can you take out of your life in order to begin anew? Whatever it may be, know that God can make it good if you trust him like Noah did. There is always a rainbow at the end of a storm – your rainbow is coming.

Surrounded By Death

Although there are rainbows at the end of a storm, I couldn't see them at the time because I felt surrounded. Death...so much death. Death in its seeming finality rose in our family like a tidal wave and completely shattered our lives. So many in my family died – literally, spiritually, emotionally, and figuratively. Our small pipe dreams, hopes, and life's wishes came crashing down around us and all we knew was the futility of struggle.

Yes, the struggle was real - more real than I imagined it would be and right before my eyes. As a small child looking at everything around me dying, I thought... *"Wow! How can I rise when everything has already died"?* My dad was dead, my step-uncle dead, my aunt, who was my favorite person in the world was diagnosed with Hodgkin's Lymphoma – dead in her thirties. My uncles, abusive and abusing their wives and others - dead. My mother's dreams - dead. My grandmother suffered from illness and depression - dead! My little life? Not started, but all this death made me feel dead too. Dead on the inside.

My father's death left an emptiness that could not be filled. I did not know it at the time, but my dad's death let me very vulnerable. It left me afraid of men. It left me needing someone to protect me and to make sure I was ok. My dad was a war hero, but the war took him away. I was left unprotected and this caused so much instability in my life that in my later years, I began to seek for protection in the wrong way. Dad's death left me to die, and inside – I did.

I died the minute they started touching me secretly. The pain of being told that I was a bad person and my mother would be hurt if I said anything made me die on the inside. The fear was crippling. I became afraid of everything. Every time a hand touched my little body and made me do things that I knew were horrific and terrible, a part of me shriveled and died. It might seem a bit much for you reader, and a little TMI, but the truth must be said and so I give it. These people made me do things a child should never experience. As a little girl of 5, I was told to touch body parts that I had not seen before. I felt like a seedling after being planted in the ground was left uncared for and the sun parched the little leaves. Without water and so much heat – it withered away. This little girl withered away and dried up even before I was 6 years old. Every time I had to place his penis in my mouth, I died. Every time he choked me with it and then urinated in my mouth and told me to swallow it, I died. Every time he laid me down and put his penis in my genitalia and rubbed against me, I died. When he made me rub his penis until he ejaculated on my face, I died. When I got sick from gonorrhea at 9 years old, I died.

I was molested for seven long years, by not one, but two people, and the fear and pain I experienced from every encounter disintegrated me into dust. It was family members who came from a father who likely did to them what they had done to me. I was dead on the inside and didn't know it. I used to wonder why no one could see what was happening to me. Even when my mom had to take me to the doctor because I became ill, she only asked me once what happened to me, and when I lied to protect her, she just let it go. At least that is what I remember. I contracted a venereal disease before I had a menstrual cycle at 9 years old, I only knew that I had to protect my mother from being harmed or harming one of them. I had to keep her alive and out of jail. What would I do if she died or went to jail because of me? This is what I thought, and so I kept my mouth shut and did what they said until I was old enough to physically fight back and I got my period and started growing breasts and could get pregnant. I don't think they wanted to risk that happening to me. So, after I told them no, and would struggle when they touched me, they left me alone. But this trauma had stolen my childhood away from me, and it caused me to go away on the inside.

What do you do with so much trauma at such a young age? I hid - I hid from everyone and everything that brought attention my way. Why did I hide? Every time I came out amongst family or friends, someone had something negative to say. I was *too much* of something all the time, and as I got older, I became tired of all the words to knock me down, so I stayed to myself and hid from them all.

I didn't know why one of my abusers would always say something if I laughed out loud at something someone said, but I would be grabbed right in front of my mom and shaken and admonished to *"Go sit down somewhere with yo' fast self"* really? I would silently ask as I walked to my room. Why would he touch me in front of them and make me a spectacle when I was only laughing? Why draw attention to the one you are abusing? Perhaps, he was gaining some sort of sexual pleasure out of shaming me in public like he shamed me in secret.

At any rate, I was a small child, had been placed in an environment that was not safe. There was no safety after my father died and really, there was no safety when he was alive because he had substance abuse issues from the Vietnam War. That war ravaged so many of our men and women and returned them to their families with broken holes…like broken cisterns in a pottery shop, veterans came back without honor and for some like my dad who lost their limbs, without wholeness and full of addictions.

~ 2 ~

THE TRAUMA OF IT ALL

"I can be changed by what happens to me. But I refuse to be reduced by it" - Maya Angelou

"Life is like a box of chocolates; you never know what you're gonna get" is a famous and often used quote from the movie Forrest Gump featuring Tom Hanks. I resonate so deeply with this character; he will probably be referenced several times throughout this story. I felt like Forrest as a child. This little girl who was crippled on the inside like Forrest's legs on the outside. Forrest was a dream maker and visionary who lived his life without apology in a world that wouldn't accept him. As a child, Forrest had his mother for his support, and her many sayings brought him through tough trials in his life. His story taught us all that anyone can come from adversity and succeed when you live your life on your terms. He was good-hearted, kind in nature, and a person that others immediately loved or hated. I related so much to Forrest because that is how people seemed to view me.

As a child, I was loved and hated, bullied and cherished, abused and encouraged to aim high. For me, it was a confusing road to travel on so young. I didn't have my mom's support like Forrest's mother was to him. His mother encouraged him to live beyond his disability and to be himself. She had a strange way of defending him, but all mothers defend their children in one way or another don't they?

My mom's defense was to teach us survival, how to fight to get what we needed accomplished, and that we could have things if we worked hard. She told us what to do but did not show us how. She worked hard yes but she never taught us about finances, how to attain wealth, or to even budget. She taught my sister and I how to cook, clean and serve our husbands. She wanted us to be the best to show others but not for ourselves.

Mom began living with a man who was an alcoholic and abuser. She met him at the hospital where she worked. He was a patient on the surgical floor. My mom had recently given her life to Christ, so she was compelled to share her salvation story with everyone she met. What better way to share her Good News than in a hospital where she worked and saw so many people.

I don't know exactly what she saw in him or what attracted her to even take the time to speak to him. I finally asked her about it now that I'm an adult and felt comfortable enough to ask her. She told me she saw him several times after that first meeting in the hospital. She had a car, so she took my aunts and her friend to a bar one evening. She said bars made her uncomfortable – probably because Grammy used to hang out with her best friend Ms. Deusa (that's what we called her) in bars. Those two women were nothing to play with. If one didn't shoot you, the other one would cut you and people knew it.

At the bar, my mom and the man who would become my step-dad saw one another and started talking, and the rest is history. He came over to our house a lot, and then he started staying over. Momma knew it was not the right thing to do in front of us kids, but she did it until the guilt settled in. I think she then confused guilt with conviction and married him eventually. She made a promise to us after my dad died that no one would come to live with us unless she married him. She said later she regretted doing that.

He took us through so much with his dysfunction. We were already a mess as a family because of the death of my dad. Now we had a man living with us who did not know how to be a father trying to care for a ready-made family. He did not have an example of how to care for kids. He came from abusive parents, and he brought that abuse into our family. He abused my mother and terrorized us as children because we were afraid that he would kill her or they would kill each other.

There was even a murder there. My stepdad was accused of killing his own brother right there in our house. His brother died outside on our concrete steps. Boy, did we become the talk of the projects then. That place was like the show *Peyton Place*...everyone knew everyone's business.

My stepdad served five out of an 18-20 year sentence for that. He said he didn't do it, and I was there. Whatever happened, it forever changed our family. My mom was at work that day, and all of us kids were home because it was Saturday. My aunt was there too. It was another confusing and sad day for all of us. After the police removed the body, we all had to leave and go to my grandmother's house. I walked down the stairs and watched my step-uncle's blood – thick and dark – run down over the concrete. There was so much blood everywhere, and it had a funny smell. It made me sick to my stomach and scared for my life. I was seven or eight years old then.

I asked mom later why she stayed with my stepdad until he died many years later of cancer. She said, she grew up in the deep South until she was nine years old with her grandparents. 'Bije' and 'Ma' as she called them, never argued, never fought one another, and she saw how they cared for one another and stood by one another through life until death. She saw their commitment and decided that she would be that committed when she married. Once my dad died, she placed that child-like committed promise on her second marriage.

Although my stepdad didn't know how to be a dad, he was good to me. He always showed me how to cook certain things, like a dessert cookie he baked in the oven called "busters." The cookie was vanilla with vanilla cream on the inside and caramel baked all around the cookie on the outside. It was so gooey and delicious! He took my family through hell, but I loved him.

Looking back on their marriage, I can definitely see the correlation of my own failed first marriage. I learned about marriage by watching my mother. I could not see and how my beliefs about marriage were the same as my mother's. I thought my commitment to being married stemmed from not wanting to be like her marriage or the marriages of my family members. But abuse is abuse, and out of abuse dysfunctional thinking is born. I was shaped by that un-natural life which became our norm.

Mom couldn't teach us what she didn't learn, so I do not blame her. I thank her for making me learn the hard life lessons I did.

A child's caregiver plays a pivotal role in normal development. Relationships, especially close relationship figures, give a child the outlet to learn trust or distrust. It teaches a child how to engage in the world and how to emotionally regulate their feelings. When close relationships are not stable, a child learns self-reliance and can develop a negative outlook on life and a distrust of others. This can play out in issues in adulthood with intimacy, friendships, and people in authority.

Post-traumatic stress disorder or PTSD is now a disorder listed in mental health books as a diagnosis for children. Back in the '70s and '80s, I did not know anything about PTSD. I did not know that I needed a child psychologist or mental health counselor to help me understand my trauma and discover healing. I was a child physically growing into an adult, but a little child in my thought process. I wondered, *"Is it possible for a person to become stuck in their childhood thinking so much so that, although as a physical adult, that person is still a naive child in the mind?"* I found that to be true in my life. Though I was becoming an adult, I had all these childlike dreams and thoughts.

I encountered so much trauma as a child. I learned to live with it. It was my normal. I didn't know that I should be living any differently except when I got lost in my books. I read so many books. I loved to read and then imagine my life like the characters I read about. I had complete collections of Nancy Drew and Hardy Boys books. I also read romance novels and poetry. I was drawn to love and mystery because I craved it for my own life. I can't say that my mother didn't love us - she did and she does. But my mother's love was always on provision and survival, keeping a roof over our heads, feeding us, having transportation for work, and making sure my siblings and I had clothes.

I hated that my mom would try to make me wear my older sister's old clothes. We were built so differently. She was petite and small, and I was big and solid. She wore a size 5 shoe, and size 3 clothes, and I was in a size 9 shoe and adult size 7 clothes at the age of 12. I remember once my mother made me wear my sister's gym suit for school. Back then we had to wear gym uniforms that looked like a onesie. It was royal blue and I felt like I looked like a stuffed blueberry. It was so tight it bunched up at the crotch choking my va-jay-jay so bad I could barely breathe. I dressed out for gym that day and when I went to run - it split all the way up the back. I was so ashamed and embarrassed, I did not dress out for gym class again for that school year, and for the first time in my life, I had an "F" on my report card. I got in trouble for that. It was the sixth grade. That was when the bullying from kids in my community really started.

Trauma has a way of changing you forever. It can reduce you to its villainy, or it can spur you to be better. Trauma can be your best friend in the victimization of it all, or it can be your worst enemy. It was both for me. I used trauma as a cloak to hide beneath when I didn't know how to come out of the coverings of everyone's derogatory spewing. I was bullied. I had to toughen up and take it where I came from. I couldn't let them see me cry and I had to fight my way out of other people's insecurities which they tried to impart to me.

Back then as a child, I didn't know that those same girls who were bullying me had their own demons to deal with. I didn't know that their self-loathing was projected onto me because I was different.

I was built differently. I matured before many of them because of the abuse I suffered but they didn't know that. All they saw was this black girl with a big booty and breasts and getting the attention from the boys because of it. They couldn't see I did not want the attention nor did I do anything to bring attention to me. It was quite the opposite. I hated that boys liked me. I hated that they wanted to do things to me that grown men had already. I was afraid of them, and I didn't want them near me. I called them my boyfriends, but really I wanted someone to hang out with and play football with and climb trees with and play our project game called *Gorman*.

The boys came and went. All that kissing behind the bushes and going up into the '*mountains*' and letting them feel on me was all a part of trying to get them to accept me. It wasn't because I liked it - I actually hated it. But I was taught from my abuse that it was a form of acceptance and love. Everywhere else I was being rejected, so I took it as love and let it be just that. I hated my body. I hated my lips because they upturn when I laugh and my top lip is large. It was a serious flaw in the mind of a pre-teen. The only part of me I loved was my mind and my eyes. My eyes told how I was feeling. They were filled with so much emotion. I think that is how those girls knew how to get to me because fear and sadness showed in my eyes.

I was twelve in the seventh grade when the humiliation took the greatest toll on me. We went to lunch, and when we came back in someone had a drawing of big lips etched into the cork board beside my desk. The caption read: *"Denise has Big lips. Denise loves Big lip Deep"* or something to that effect. Deep - as he was so aptly named because of the dark, rich color of his skin - was a boy in my class that liked me. We lived in the same projects, just on different sides of the community. We were the second or third year generation of black kids who were integrated into this public school on the

White side of town. The first was my older brother's class who was integrated there in the first set of Black and Latino children into this school.

I think Deep and I liked one another because we were different and because we were talked about the most. Someone always had something ugly to say about us. He was the nicest person to me. He had the nicest brother and sisters. I was glad to know them. I was picked on by the popular project girls. They made fun of me and taunted me for a few years. I tried to be friends with them, but it never worked out. I tried to hang out and talk about other people when they did, but when it got back to the person talked about, my name was the only name mentioned. I had several fights because of these girls. But I never backed down. Scared or not. I put Vaseline on my face to get ready for any punches and so my face couldn't get scratched up, and I went out there to face my giants literally. I hated everything about being black and living in those projects.

So, when I went to high school, I found my tribe: the Puerto Rican community. Those girls had your back, and when they called you friend, you were a friend. I left my own people to join another who were more my people, and it felt good! I was accepted - even when there was a miscommunication We cleared it up, squashed it, and were girls again. They looked out for me, and I looked out and appreciated them.

That's when I met my guy. He was Puerto Rican and fine! I was glad the Puerto Rican community accepted me. They made me feel as if I was their own, and it felt good to be accepted and not rejected for the first time in my life. I fell in love with them and was so happy to be a part of them. I learned that certain Hispanic people didn't hang with others. The Italians hung with Italians, the Blacks with the Blacks, the Hispanics though, they had their own tribes within their ethnicity, and it was interesting to see. I guess it was kind of like the issue the black community in the '60s and '70s had with the lighter skinned versus the darker skinned - like who is better. It's called colorism. We are the same in the eyes of others, but we act like the tone of skin determined whether or not you were a better black person. Crazy how we think as a nation and a society of people.

In the beginning of my junior year of high school, one of the girls from the projects and I who were friends began to have beef over some 'he-say-she-say' stuff. Now, mind you, I could care less about those girls who stirred up trouble in the projects because I had my tribe, but this girl who had a beef with me over a boy again - was a friend. So, when I told my tribe what was going on, they had my back. This girl and I were supposed to fight after the last class at the "head." The statue of John F. Kennedy was in front of the high school with the same name, and that is where we were supposed to meet and fight. So, the kids from the projects knew all about it, and my tribe knew. I was fed up, and I had backing, so I went there to do what I knew I had to do. Turned out that neither one of us really wanted to fight. It was all a misunderstanding. We settled it and I walked home. Shortly after that incident, my family moved away to the South.

Moving to the South was so difficult for me. I was 17, in the last year and a half of high school, and I wanted to finish school in New Jersey. Mom thought it was best to move us, so we went. The South brought so many other things to my life. Teen pregnancy, teen marriage, twenty years of life with a man who resented and used me.

I moved south and that is where I met my ex-husband. He was a guy who saw me walking to the store one day and offered me a ride. He was a senior in high school and I thought that he seemed like someone I could probably become friends with. I didn't give him the time of day at first. He drove this big tan colored LTD and he was very short so he looked so funny in that car. I began talking to him and found that we could talk about many things. He was traveled because his family was military and he had lived in other places. He was intelligent and he knew how to get high! So, I began dating him. I got pregnant in my senior year of high school and had a miscarriage. Another death in my young life. It was very hard to get through, not only because of the loss of the baby, but the pressure I was getting from family. My mom wanted me to break up with him, and he was telling me his mom disapproved of us living together. They called it 'shacking'. I was from the North and we 'shacked' all the time. I wasn't about to get married at 17!

I graduated from high school and my mom thought it best to send me back to NJ to go to college. She wanted me as far away from my boyfriend as possible. She did not want anything or anyone to deter me from success. I did not say earlier, but my boyfriend gave me a ring for engagement at 17. We were from the north and did not believe in being engaged that young, but my mom let me keep the ring anyway.

Not all the years were bad, but there were many that were. Married seventeen years and been with him for 3 years prior, my life was taken away again before it could start. All my dreams of being an IBM executive washed away as soon as I met him. There were a lot of things which transpired that pushed me into his arms, but the main point I want to make here is that I was a baby having a baby and marrying a baby. I went to college majoring in Pre-Nursing and hated it. It was her dream - not mine. I remember sitting in the cafeteria at the college one day thinking to myself: "W*hat is my purpose? Why was I born? What was I born to become?"* Have you ever asked yourself this question? I did, and it made me sad, because I really didn't know. It took me many years to finally see what I was born for. So many years of going through so much to come to a place of *being free.*

Life Lesson #2 – *Understanding Your Purpose is Freedom*

Recently while attending an online women's Bible Study, the women were asked if they knew their purpose, and sadly many did not. When I asked myself that purpose question so many years ago, I was unaware it would mean so much to me now. We know our purpose here is to glorify God with our lives, but when you've had a life which brought shame and uncertainty, how does God get glory from that? I was entering college when that question entered my heart and I didn't know how to answer it. I began a search on what purpose is, and when life happened, I stopped. I lived how I was raised - to survive and not thrive.

In retrospect, I see that everything which transpired up until this point had a purpose. Although some events brought sadness and shame, I know now that it all worked together for good. God knew that I would give my life to him and he certainly knew the struggles I would have along the way. As I began to understand that everything in my life has a purpose, I was able to gain freedom in my heart in areas where I felt condemnation and shame. God doesn't condemn, Satan does. God doesn't shame – it is sin which brings shame. Knowing this helped me to understand and to be set free from my past.

Eve had a purpose and God outlined her purpose in the first chapter of Genesis. He said:

> *God created human beings; he created them godlike, reflecting God's nature. He created them male and female. God blessed them: "Prosper! Reproduce! Fill Earth! Take charge! Be responsible for fish in the sea and birds in the air, for every living thing that moves on the face of Earth. (Genesis 1:27, 28 – The MSG)*

Eve's purpose was clearly stated by God. She was to bear fruit and rule the Earth with her partner Adam. She failed and brought shame into the Earth when she disobeyed God's command. She was deceived by the serpent and both she and Adam brought a curse upon mankind. However, Eve still prospered and became free when she discovered her purpose in bearing her children. She saw how her shame had consequences when her son Cain killed his brother Abel because he was jealous, but she also saw how her shame brought triumph when she bore Seth her third son. Seth's name means "compensation". He was a type of Christ, who would be provided as compensation for the sins of man and would set us free as we accept Him as Lord of our lives.

So it is with you. Your past has a pass. Jesus died to save you from the condemnation and guilt of this world and to set you on a life path of freedom and blessing in him. He certainly has done this for me. Today, will you accept him? It comes with believing He is God's Son and accepting his death, burial, resurrection, and enthronement in Heaven. He is here for you. Ask him to make you free and he will. He did it for me, and he will do it for you.

~ 3 ~

THE CAVED BIRD SET FREE

"The caged bird sings with a fearful trill of things unknown but longed for still and his tune is heard on the distant hill for the caged bird sings of freedom" - Maya Angelou

Freedom is a word that I do not take lightly. I come from a people who were enslaved for over 400 years, and still, my people suffer from a different form of slavery. It's called systemic racism. So many men and women have gone before me to fight for freedom for Black people. They suffered loss, had limbs taken, children beaten, and were sold to other slave owners. They suffered lynching, rapes, sodomy, tarring, and any and all terrors that whites could inflict upon this people all because of the color of our skin.

Why do people think we are less because our skin is a different shade? Why choose us to belittle, to profile, to defile, to keep us caved in the darkness of their own blackened hearts? As I think about what freedom really means and what being authentic and true to myself is, I look back over my life, and can now see in many ways where I felt caved in or stuck in my journey from the plagues of racism.

I was caved in my mind. Negative thoughts plagued me, sending me through a spiral of emotions. It kept me feeling rejection, dejection, no self-love, and a loathing for the skin I am in. My mind

- indoctrinated by the whims of White America via media, societal norms, and growing up in an era of segregation into integration - kept me stuck and told me I was less than. I was less than to my Latin-American associates, I was less than my Italian-American friends, I was less than my African-born, Caribbean-born friends. I was sub-zero to the Asians and even lesser than that to White Americans. TV led me to believe that I had to wait in the back of the line to gain a small piece of the pie...when in actuality, I was eating the crumbs of the pie from the earth from where we all derived. I felt like I had to meet the expectations of others. Being caged in made me feel as though I had no rights to ownership over my life. I was not the captain of my ship, and I let other people's opinions steer me in any direction they wanted me to go. I was tossed and confused and lost and abused. I thought I was a victim of my circumstance, not understanding that my lack of understanding proper boundaries allowed people to dictate my life.

Children are made to be free spirits. We are made as human beings to dream, to imagine, to ask for everything from the world and have the innate ability, drive, and courage to expect it and to go after it. It comes from the stage in our psychosocial learning which makes us selfish enough to want it and bold enough to demand it. Erik Erikson calls this stage initiative vs. guilt. In this stage a normal developing child gains the understanding that the world is a place to be trusted and this child gains initiative to act more independently. This age of 3 -5 years old is a time where a normal developing child explores his or her abilities. This is dreaming time and the development of ambition and direction. In this stage as well, children want to make their own choices and parents should allow it with safe boundaries established and modeling with positive reinforcement. Successful completion of this stage in a child leads to a sense of purpose. What happens though when the opposite occurs?

A child who fails to receive the proper nurturing in this stage does not develop normal initiative. Instead, the child develops fear.

The child can also foster feelings of guilt, become fragile emotionally, and will detach. If a child fails in this stage to develop proper initiative or dares to dream, He or she is made to feel as if they are wrong and may be left with abnormal guilt and a sense of rejection. This is what happened to me. As a result of childhood sexual trauma, I was forced to go into the cave. What is the cave? It is a place one retreats to inside with caverns and caverns of dark places. In these dark places, one can hide. I became very good at hiding. I was so good at it that I hid from myself. I retreated so far into the dark that I no longer knew how to find *me*.

The dark place is also a place of fear. The place where the dark overtakes the soul of the child, and he or she is too afraid to come out. That is where my childhood ended. How old was I? Five. Being forced in the cave discouraged growth in other areas of my psyche (soul). My psychosocial growth was halted at age five, and I did not realize I was still there in my heart until I reached the age of thirty.

I did not act like a child, for I had children of my own, but my dreams died or rather they were hidden in the cave so I did not know who I was. Deep in the cavern of my emotional self, I was without identity.

So how did I identify? Through my environment. I became a chameleon, and whatever made others happy I did, so I could identify with them because I could not identify with myself. I did not know that I was trying to gain an identity. I only knew that I had to be relatable, and if that was identity, then I was all for it.

My 'self' became a place for others to gain and me to serve. I became a slave to opinions and was mastered by them. I allowed the words of others to shape and form my life.

In middle school, my mother would tell me that I was going to become a doctor because I was intellectually smart. So, what did I do? I studied more and read so many books because I wanted to make her happy. Cave number one. What child does not want to make her mom proud right? If the kids in the projects where we lived called me names because of the way I looked, I believed them and tried to cover up by wearing clothing that hid my body. Cave number two. I related to the story of the Ugly Duckling so much...but I wasn't sure that one day I would turn into a beautiful swan. I only hoped.

I matured faster than girls my age, and my shoe size 9 in the sixth grade was too big. So, in order to be relatable, I tried to squeeze my feet in a size 8 to be like them. Other girls received attention if their hair was straight, so because I didn't know how to do my hair and I thought I was too old for cornrows (my sister hated braiding my hair), I tried to do it myself. That was a disaster, and my mom took me to the barber and shaved off all my hair. Cave number three. Deeper in the cavern I went after that. I was bullied so badly because of that.

In the deep recesses of those caves, I discovered something I could do and which I began to do with passion. I wrote. I read poetry books by Elizabeth Barrett Browning. I realized in her words that I could live there. I would escape every day in novels and poetry and imagine myself there interacting with the characters in those pages. There were no caves there. There I was free. There I was myself.

But was I? Wasn't I using the world of prose to escape and become there what I thought in my mind was acceptance by the characters? Of course, I was, but it was far better to be in a world of aristocrats than to be in the world I lived in. Some would call it daydreaming but I called it my oasis. It was my way of escape, and I took it.

I remember the first time I read African American poetry. The depth of feeling and emotion in every word of every poem spoke and still speaks volumes to my spirit and my soul. There is one poem in particular which reached the deepest places in my cave. It was a poem by the late and great Maya Angelou. It was *"I Know Why the Caged Bird Sings."* This poem has meant so much to me because the bird was me, but I was not in a cage - I was in a cave. In the cage the bird could see and long for the things it fearfully desired, but not me. I couldn't see anything, for I was in darkness and the cave though a place I lived and often retreated to throughout my life, was also a prison.

In the cage the bird could still sing although his wings were clipped and his feet were tied. I could enter and leave the cave, but it was so dark and there were so many caverns, I couldn't see or simply walk out. I couldn't sing because my voice was stolen and in its place…the voices of others. *"No one would hear me"* the voices would taunt, and I believed them.

The poems I read became my voice. The poems spoke to my pain. The poems became my salvation until one day I read another set of poems. These poems and those words became light in the caverns of my soul. Its poetic beauty illuminated my heart and captured me. it was the Bible and the Word saved me. He set me free when I read these words:

> *I am the Vine; you are the branches. When you're joined with me and I with you, the relation intimate and organic, the harvest is sure to be abundant. Separated, you can't produce a thing. Anyone who separates from me is deadwood, gathered up and thrown on the bonfire. But if you make yourselves at home with me and my words are at home in you, you can be sure that whatever you ask will be listened to and acted upon. This is how my Father shows who he is—when you produce grapes, when you mature as my disciples"* (John 15:5-8 MSG)

I saw through the reading of the Scriptures that I meant something to someone and that God who formed me before I was even born knew me and wanted me. He was my home. This was a revelation and a wonder to my soul. It began the lighted path to my release and my inner healing. I was dead without him, but with him, I could be abundant. I clung to those words and I came alive. I was 30 years old and had so much inner trauma and pain from my past, but inside, I knew that this was my answer.

~ 4 ~

MARRIAGE MATTERS – A POEM

"The ultimate purpose of marriage is not to make us happy, but to glorify God" - Nancy Leigh DeMoss

It started when I divorced from my first marriage. It was my choice and due to his infidelity. The divorce taught me so much about myself and so much about other people. I've always wanted to be married. From a small child it was a dream of mine. I would play in my Tuesday Taylor dollhouse and dream that my life would be like the family I dreamed of. I think this type of dreaming was my way out of the dark hole I was living in. My childhood was a dark place and I wanted to escape. So, I got married at the age of 19. I was a child.

As I went through my first marriage I took those childhood dreams and tried to make them my reality. They didn't come true because I failed to understand that the man I married was not the person I saw in my dreams. He was totally different. He was not the rescuer, the succorer, the protector that I read about in those romance novels. He was a real person, with his own issues who needed to grow up just like I did. We both were children who entered a sacred space as children and like a child who enters a clean house with muddy feet, we made a big mess!

We tried to make the marriage work at first. We tried to be to one another what we could be. We did love one another, and still today I have a platonic love towards him and will always care deeply for him; but I do know that he was not the person, nor was I the person, to marry. I took what I saw as a child and tried to make that abuse turn into a fairy tale. I was committed to the term marriage but did not really understand what real marriage was about. I had my faults too. I was too immature to handle marriage, and as I changed, we grew apart. I instead tried to keep the marriage together. We tried to be for one another what we thought was right. We tried to be better than those who had relationships around us, but really we had no real example of marriage from which to draw. So instead, I dreamed. The marriage failed, but I still continued to dream. That dreaming was my escape. Those dreams turned into one failed relationship after another. I was still searching for something outside of me when the real answer was within. The poem of sorts below is what I learned.

All this time I've been watching in my mind, the things I've been looking forward to
The things I've wanted since the day I could dream those little girlish dreams of youth.
I've dreamt of picket fences, dogs a running, a little child, and a home with a husband by my side.
I've dreamt of a career and a home with no fear, and a lavish wedding no girl would turn aside.
I've dreamt that my husband and I would even die side-by-side on a sunset evening rocking in our swings.

That even until death would we part - and nothing would come between - nothing would deter me from my dreams.
Yet this little girl's dream kept getting shattered on repeat as she tried to create what she saw.

The house came and went, the kids grew up and left, and the husband - in name only was now gone.

What happened to my rainbow in the sky?
Did I cry as I sat shattered, bewildered, hurt and forlorn?
I looked and I tried and I tried and I cried but couldn't find my rainbow in the sky.

So, now the little girl gone is a woman with no home and the same dream ruminating in her mind
tried to recreate the dream once again, but still torn apart inside.
Now to fit the time and age where she was and what she made; this woman-little girl got back on her carpet ride.

I prayed and I asked God to show me the guy that I could call my only one
so, I began to learn what marriage was.
Funny thing though happened then - instead of God showing me a man,
He began to show me how marriage represented Him.
I studied and became fascinated with this thing that I began to look for "Mr. Marry" that same way!

I'm in church and praying hard and making a list and checking it twice
and here comes "Mr. Perfect - Mr. Preacher - Mr. Right"...or so I thought.
I waited and waited three years later for God to make us perfect and let him know I was his wife.
He and I began a conversation on the phone and I even made him a robe to preach in - here I go - investing in someone who wasn't "the one".
Instead of being a real man and giving the gift back because he had other plans, he played my heart and made me appear as a fool.

I was hurt and disillusioned to the point of utter confusion and still God said nothing about discontinuing - after a bit of healing I moved on.

I enrolled in dating sites, got scammed by this African man who was more than two thousand miles away.

Here I go a-giving again - and as he even once said, "I shot myself" - for others who invested in my false dream.

I got tried, then met a guy I thought could be a possibility but found out he went to jail.

I even wrote to him and found out after a short time he got out and needed a little "Joe time" to himself.

After leaving that one alone and seeking God again for the one, I met through my sister's dating site a guy named Rick.

"Slick Rick" as someone called him turned out to be "Sick Rick" as I unfolded, because he was clinically depressed,

not over his first marriage and non-committed.

He played with my heart because he had me from the start thinking he was marriage-minded and ready to go on.

Then all of sudden, "God couldn't possibly want him to marry because he divorced without the cause of adultery on her part".

After I got him to seek therapy, and to get on medication and to work out his body again physically

He got well and he got married - so apparently - God did want him to marry...well maybe but just not to me.

Here I go a-chasing after rainbows and after two rings: one to engage myself in a committed relationship and one to bind me in matrimony

and all the while God was waiting in the wings.

I kept going and I kept looking and the devil came pursuing.

Never did I think in a million years I would do something so demeaning and hideous as to engage in sin.

But I did and I involved myself with a married man - yes, I said it and I did - so stone me if you will.

Ahhh!!! The room is quiet because now I'm not looked upon with pity but with dislike and disdain. What a bitter pill!

How could you? Some are thinking...*no wonder you were where you are,* some are saying...and *My God!!*

The shame! others are saying amongst other things.

Don't think I haven't said those same things myself when I learned about women like me who were standing where I'm standing at today.

How did I get here? Why did I do this? Did I break up his marriage?

I'm ashamed but the little girl in me desperate was crying to be held and to gain some attention from any man.

I judged and am now being judged. The girl code was broken and I could never return from this degradation...but girl code or not,

I was wrong for engaging in a marriage when it was not my place.

Funny thing is I will never again judge someone on the basis of outward information before I know the full story

because that is what God taught me with my own dream.

There is a story in the Bible about a woman named Gomer and a man named Hosea who married her

There is a story in the Bible about a woman who was caught in the act of adultery and Jesus rescued her from those who would have her stoned.

Before you pick up your stones to throw at me, make sure that is what the Lord wants you to do, and then pick up your own.

As I continue chasing my rainbow, this man whom I'm now involved, began living in the same home.

I was ridiculed and I looked bad in front of my family and my friends, and even in front of those girls I mentored.

I was leveled to the ground with guilt over the break-up of a marriage which was done way before I came onto the scene.

I was made the scapegoat and this man's ex was an evangelist and she went for the jugular in the courts.

She dragged the proceedings on for months and then years, so I began to wonder, "God, what is happening to my rainbowed life?"

I cried and I cried...I can hear someone saying now it is well-deserved, but no one deserves such crushing,

but I did and I do deserve to crush this little girl dream I created - it was not from God.

God did show me a rainbow one day as a covenant between Him and I and He reminded me of it several times.

Then this morning when I woke the rainbow came again and I was reminded I was chasing the wrong rainbow in the sky.

My rainbow is not a marriage, it is not two rings, or a man. My rainbow is not over giving, or over investing in anyone or anything.

My rainbow is not in hiding myself and not being who I really am. My rainbow is not pleasing everybody so that they will find acceptance in me.

My rainbow is not my dream house, or a car, or dogs running or picket fences - I've had those things.

My rainbow is not in finding validation in my career, or in the people who I work for or who work for me.

My rainbow is not feeling guilty for committing fornication or having an affair with a married man.

My rainbow is not in pleasing his every whim or his every move or in trying to ensure he will never cheat again.

My rainbow is my covenant with my God and His covenant with me.

My rainbow is to myself to allow myself the air to breathe - the life to live - the chance to see all that He wants for me.

My covenant is to be truly the 'Me' I was born to be without fault, or fear, or doubt, or excuse, or compromise, or pretense, or shame.

I can no longer worry about what a little girl dreamt over fifty years ago.

I now must look forward to who I am, what I want, and how I wear my coat of many colors.

Although many may disdain me for getting my coat, I have it nonetheless and I - I shall wear it and wear it well, no I'm not going to hell,
  but I see that marriage matters - my marriage to God.

This is my story, this is my strength, and this is my song. God is not through with me -
  He is simply releasing my rainbow, so I can be seen.

A rainbow is beautiful and when it is in the sky, it is noticed and all admire its beauty.
   It's not shiny, it's distinct, and beautiful in its own right.
  Every rainbow has its own hue and its own way to hang in the sky, but it is there and it is one seen by all.
  I am ready to be seen by all for my rainbow came after my storm. I no longer chase the rainbow I wear it for it's my covenant - I truly belong to God.

~ 5 ~

THE CROSS I MADE

*"Then Jesus went to work on His disciples. "Anyone who intends to come with me has to let me lead. You're not in the driver's seat; I am. Don't run from suffering; embrace it. Follow **me** and I'll show you how. Self-help is no help at all. Self-sacrifice is the way, my way, to finding yourself, your true self. What kind of deal is it to get everything you want but lose yourself? What could you ever trade your soul for? " - Matthew 16:24-26 – MSG*

I had a dream that I was in fright or fight or flight mode. I wasn't exactly sure, but the feelings and the emotions attached to the dream made it so real that I awoke in full emotional turmoil. I felt like the dream was prophetic, telling me that something was about to change. It was concerning my second marriage.

In order to give you the breakdown of my previous chapter's poem, I am going to share with you my life with men, the relationships I've had, my two marriages and my takeaways from it. I hope that you glean something from the mess of me and I hope in some of these paragraphs you will laugh with me and cry with me and be with me on this journey in openness and truth. Maybe you will find something relatable, maybe you won't, but come along with me anyway. I think you'll find my truth and lessons learned interesting.

One day as I was sitting at work, the Holy Spirit spoke to me and told me to write. This is what he said,

"Now that you have the man, you are still so incomplete, and now you fear making any sacrifice to change what you have done for guilt's sake. Why do you hold onto guilt that serves you no purpose under the sun? To make yourself seem right in the eyes of a man. You don't have to be obligated to someone I did not match you with. For the second time, you have chosen someone for you - I did not choose him - you did. What God has put together let not man put asunder. So, you work hard to keep it by distancing yourself from it. Huh? You say? Yes - you distance your heart from this man so if it doesn't turn out well, you can go through the pain easier. But really you are shielding yourself from really feeling anything.

You want to know something? Since you were molested you never really knew what true love is like. You felt the desperation of emotional love that has strings attached to it. And you have that same love with your husband. You love him out of obligation to your guilt - the same way you loved your first husband out of obligation to the commitment of marriage. Both wrong reasons and not real love, and both to prove a point. You want to know what's really wrong with you? You don't know real love, and because of that you can't know My love towards you. You are numb to love because you numbed your heart as you numbed your body as a little girl from the shame of being you. The enemy shamed you into a cave, and you have lived your life in there ever since.

When you get a glimpse of freedom, you come and stick a toe out, but the minute you sense danger for your heart - you go back inside, not realizing you cannot really recognize real danger because your inner sight is tainted. Your heart, little one, is crushed. You have hidden behind sexuality, sadness, intelligence, and masking because that is what people recognize you for - helping and servanthood (in the slave sense), and for your gift of prophecy when they need a word. Your husband (partner) does not even know who you are, and if you ask, he will tell you only surface things because he is too self-absorbed and dysfunctional to recognize your heart. Instead of being sad about where you think you are - be glad that you see it and look forward to being better.

Becoming the woman, you see inside - the woman you visualize is going to take a lot of change. A lot of soul-searching and a big release in your own life of the fears that have kept you bound for so long. I know who you are, but you don't, and I know that you are sad about that, but I Am here to tell you that you are more than you see and greater than you dreamed. In you the keys to your life are being held. In you are the keys to every door of opportunity you have prayed about and to doors unknown. In you are the seeds to the treasure of your life that you have been looking for. You have to reach inside and find them. It's not hard. You need to clear your heart and mind and it will happen. You ask how? When you spend time with me. Not seeking me for a mate or seeking me to find out what you are to do next; but simply seeking me."

Wow right? I was blown away by what the Holy Spirit spoke into my heart, because it was such a dilemma inside of me for so long. Maybe you want to know how I could hear him so clearly when I could not before? I can say that it was simply because I was seeking him for answers. I needed to desperately hear from the Lord, so I spent time inside searching for him. How did I search? I quieted down my mind, I centered my heart in stillness, and I prayed. I sought His Word. Every chance I had, I continued in this way to speak to the Lord. I waited on His voice - the inner voice I knew was not mine. He has a distinct way of letting you know it is him speaking. I waited patiently, and He heard me. I'm so glad He did tell me.

I went through so many things in my past, I became hardened over time without realizing it. After going through so much, I became very selfish. I wanted what I wanted, and didn't care because, I was hurting. In those first months of being with my current husband, all I desired was his company. He and I were friends first. We reconnected on social media. For months we just developed a friendship and a closeness that I recognized as easy. For the first time in my life, I was comfortable being around a man, so I latched on to him like a hungry baby sucking her mother's breast. Subconsciously, I was concerned that he had a family. I felt rejected from the past for so long that I wanted recompense and I took what he offered me. I knew from the beginning of our meeting on Facebook that he was married and what began in the first months as becoming more acquainted as friends turned into something so much more. I believed he accepted me as I was, and he treated me as if I mattered.

After a while had gone by, it did begin to matter. It mattered a lot. My heart ached for him, and I was ashamed before God, my family, and those who knew about us. I knew silently that I was being judged, and that I deserved every unkind word or thought spoken to me and about me. I was plagued with guilt, and the enemy battered my mind with condemning words.

I said it all to myself. I didn't want to get married after being in that situation with him for a year. I only wanted what was best, but we had gone too far and hurt too many people to turn back. We knew it too and tried to make the best of it. I told him to go back and work it out with his family several times because the guilt was so strong, but he insisted that it would never be the same, and she would never take him back. In my heart I believed that was a lie. I believed she still loved him and she probably would never marry again. I was wrong for stepping in the way, even though he justified his desire to leave her, and God dealt with me very seriously about it. After years of no communication, I sent her flowers under the guise of an anonymous secret sister.

I wanted to say I was sorry for what I did, but that was not enough. God told me to get it right, and so I wrote her a letter and mailed it. I acknowledged my part in the destruction of her family, and I apologized with every fiber of my being for hurting her and her children. I didn't want a response nor did I want her to accept it. I knew I had to repent before God, and my repentance meant acknowledging my wrong. After the divorce she was very civil to him – even when he was horrible to her. When he did things to upset her, the kids knew about it. It caused them to be estranged for many years. It showed me her pain, her love, and her devastation. Everyone has their Achilles heel, and my husband was hers.

I don't know where they are now with their level of civility but some of his adult children are back in relationship with him, and for that I am so grateful. I know what that pain is like. It happened to me in my first marriage and was the reason I divorced. You are asking yourself right now, *"Then if you knew how it felt, why in the world would you do that to someone else, and you say you are a Christian?"* I know. I am saved; but I was broken…a very broken woman.

When I was going through betrayal in my first marriage, I said that I would never want anyone to feel the pain and devastation I felt when it happened to me. My children were small then, and they felt my ex-husband had abandoned them, but I tried to make the best of a very bad situation. When you are in a failing marriage everyone in the household has very different views of divorce, and every view is according to that individual and therefore their truth. My view was that I was lost, rejected again, and devastated. I knew my children would change their feelings about their dad, and in some ways they have, some for good, and some because he is their dad.

With a few of my current husband's adult children, I knew immediately what they felt about me. They have made it crystal clear. I don't blame them. Little did they know I received their words and wore them around my neck like a beaded necklace for so many years. I was so sorry for what I did to them. It took years, and on again off again types of conversations with their dad, but I believed and secretly prayed that they would be reunited and for good, and God is still working, and for that I am grateful.

I love my husband. I loved him when we first met (or so I thought it was love). He was easy to fall for. He is a laid-back, simple man with a very multifaceted inner being. He is complicated but tries not to be and he doesn't like to complicate things, yet he always manages to. He always says he is a *"plain meat and potatoes guy"* and he is, yet he isn't.

There is a side to this man that is so beautifully haunted. He won't tell you the deep side to his heart, you just know it's there. He won't ask for much, but there is a side to him that seeks much in return, and I am drawn to that and exhausted with that at the same time. He was so beautiful to me in the beginning – but aren't they all like that when they are wooing you? When we were adjusting to the relationship and waiting for his divorce to become final, we were living together, and he cheated on me. His infidelity was a trigger in my heart from my past and it was a very difficult season for both of us. When we met, I told him about my past and how deeply it affected me, but because I entered this relationship on those same factors, he did not take me seriously, and felt like he could do what he had done previously in his first marriage.

My heart was broken in two. Not only because I sinned against God, but I was fornicating, and I was dealing with that. On top of this, I felt as though he didn't care for my feelings and what I felt I had given up for him. I deserved it, yes, and I considered leaving the relationship. I had to leave town for a few days to clear my head, so my best friend sent me a plane ticket and I went to visit with her. During those days there, I really went before the Lord to seek Him. This, of course, was my way out of this mess I created right?

I tried to justify my sin before the Lord under the guise of my pain, but God was not having it. He spoke to me very clearly about my part in my pain and gave me instructions to seek Him more. I did not have an answer to end the relationship, so I went home and sought the Lord more. Karma was returning the favor to me that I gave out and I definitely reaped what I had sown, but what was the answer? After fasting and sleeping in another space in our home for a while to hear the Lord clearly, I strongly felt the Lord tell me to remain. It sounded crazy to me and I know a lot of you will say that I was not hearing correctly, but I did. I know God did not choose that relationship for me – I did that, but it was God who knew the future and what life would bring, and it is God who knows the hearts of men. I listened – even though I wanted to end the relationship, and we worked through it. How did we work through it? My obedience. I submitted myself to the Lord every single day. I was hurt, but I could not concentrate solely on the emotions I was experiencing. Instead, I focused on God. I prayed continually and remained quiet. I chose to forgive myself, and I chose to forgive him. I chose to be still and know that God is God and allowed Him the space to deal with the things in my heart I was having issues with.

I was feeling quite guilty, and I was not desperate for a relationship anymore. After going to my husband and talking it though, we decided to remain together with a clear understanding of both of our expectations of the relationship. I expected God to help me, and for my husband to be accountable going forward, and he expected me to forgive him. So, I did, and after his divorce, we married.

Yes girl, I know you are hollering at this point and saying: *"You a fool!"* and you're right in a sense. A foolish woman does the things I did and a woman who is broken and bereft of real love will take whatever is given, even if it is not truth. I knew that he was the type of man who was not faithful because he was not faithful in his first marriage. At that time in his life, he was unparalleled in the lack of self-discipline and self-control. Nothing would stop him if he really wanted it. If only he could have turned that energy into the marriage more...he would get on his train and ride...and sometimes, I rode it out with him and sometimes, I would let him ride alone. He has a beautiful mind – for it works in a complex manner.

In many ways I felt like I deserved the treatment I received from him, because of my part in the dissolution of his marriage. I knew that he was in his own way trying to love. Yet that was not real love. How could he love me when truly he didn't love himself? No person with genuine self-love could be out in the streets like he was and hurt so many as he did. Jesus tells husbands to love their wives as Christ loves the church and gave Himself for it...He tells them to love their wives as they do their own bodies. I knew my husband didn't love himself, so he could not really love me until he learned this. I knew this, but I resigned to hang on the cross I made and pray until I saw change...and I did. It began with me. God began to deal with my heart to make wrong things right.

When people say that God is dealing with them, it can mean many things. For me, it meant that the Holy Spirit presented to me in my heart things which were not right. Some could call it consciousness of sin. I knew that in order to walk in truth about my own life in this area, I had to acknowledge first to myself and then to God that I was the cause of my pain. I was messed up in this area and I needed his help. I repented and I asked God's forgiveness and he placed me on a road to self-discovery and showed me mercy and his love. What did he do, and how did he help me? He reminded me of how I felt when I was betrayed, and he began to show me through the Word of God his thoughts about me. He reminded me that I was chosen. He reminded me that I was accepted. He reminded me that He had a plan for my life and that more than all of that, he – if no one else – loved me he does.

Jeremiah 1:5 says:

> *Before I formed you in the womb I knew you*
> *[and approved of you as My chosen instrument],*
> *And before you were born I consecrated you*
> *[to Myself as My own]; I have appointed you as*
> *a prophet to the nations.* (AMP)

I knew then that God had a plan for my future and for my life far greater than I ever imagined. I knew that he wanted me and that he loved me because he created me for a purpose. I knew that whatever happened to me in my past as a result of other people's bad decisions towards me and my own decisions towards myself, could not deter what God had created me for. If I would turn to Him only, He would bring me to a place of healing and real purpose and peace.

As for my husband and me? We are still together. We are happily married seven years. We traveled this rocky road and had major bumps along the way. I did not reveal to him how I felt about my guilt until several years after we married and I had apologized to his ex-wife. He was surprised, and as we discussed it, he saw a part of my heart that he had not noticed before, and I saw his softer side. He has changed. He is accountable to this marriage, and he holds me in a sacred place. He is more understanding and he listens to what I am saying from my heart. He has matured in ways I could not imagine, and I can tangibly see the results of my prayers. We were always friends, and because of our friendship, we have a respect and ease with one another which makes communication better. I humbled myself and placed this relationship in God's Hands, and He worked it out. My husband had to see Jesus in me, not my old hurts and scathing words. He had to see God's love, and that has made all the difference. Was it easy? NO! We have worked through the adjustment period of marriage *after* we came through the hardness of his divorce and relationship with his children. Those years were very tough. I really had to lean on the Lord to help me not to walk away. He wanted to end things as well. But God kept telling me to stay. He told me that my husband needed me, and I needed to trust Him through this process. My husband now prays with me, and we make our decisions together. We have our days like anyone else, but we have each other's best interest at heart. Ecclesiastes 3:11 says, *He has made everything beautiful and appropriate in its time,* and God has done that with my marriage.

This journey was difficult to say the least, but we have turned a corner and we are solid. We truly can say we love each other dearly, and he and I are becoming one. Now those who are religious would probably not agree with me. God is so much greater than religion speaks of Him. God has so many ways in which He prunes us and teaches us. He used my choices to make me and my husband submit. I submitted myself to God and was then able to submit myself to my husband. My husband saw God's love working through me and in turn submitted himself to me. This is where we are and if I had listened to religious teachers who say that adultery and fornication are the ultimate sin and make you feel as though you cannot come back from that, I would still be in a mess and probably divorced for the second time. I could no longer remain in religion. It was partly my fault for believing rules and doctrines of men, but in any case I am blessed that God brought me out of that.

I had left organized religion over ten years and was not going back to that. Let me also say church as an organizational institution is fine for anyone who desires that, but I wanted more: I wanted God and the kingdom of God, and I wanted to be around his people worshipping in Spirit and truth – not religious rules and doctrines of men. I do fellowship with other believers and He has made a way for me to do so, yet it is not the same as before. My fellowship now with other believers is the Kingdom of God and there is a difference. We are a living breathing organism - the Body, not just a building made with hands. But just because my life in organized institutions was over, did not mean that my life with God my Maker was over. In fact, it was really just beginning! God had a plan for me, and he made me just so I could complete that plan. I was not happy, and I knew when he led me to that Scripture in Jeremiah chapter 1, I could hope again. God had revealed to me my brokenness, and led me through His love towards victory.

I was not healed from my past, no matter how many times I went into a church, did church work, and shouted over the pain - I was not healed. He allowed me to move away and venture into the wilderness of my own soul to see what was really there. He allowed me to go to the lowest points of myself so I could see me - the dirty, low down me. I went to the pit where my heart dwelled, and even though I knew I was saved in word. I became really saved indeed. I saw the darkness of my heart and I hated what I saw. I could not justify the truth, I had to come to accept it, own it, and own up to it before God. I wanted to do right and I wanted to be right, but my rightness or my righteousness was filthy before a True and Living God, and He had to show me that.

At first I didn't want to face myself (conscious). I wanted to justify it with Scripture, with excuses for another person's behavior. I wanted to blame it on my childhood trauma, my first marriage, and all the pain I went through with that, but the truth...the real truth is that my heart was not dealt with in the first place. It was covered over with works and words and gifts that God had given me. I could work my gifts with a broken heart. I could work in the church with all that darkness inside and God did anoint what I did in the church and in my work because "the gifts and callings of God are irrevocable." (Romans 11:29) He came as Jesus and worked with his disciples in their darkness and brokenness. He went through the wilderness as an example and led them and then he gave them the fire. He has done the same for me. He gave me the gifts for His glory, but I was using the gifts to cover my dirty story.

We are all hurt people when we first accept Jesus as our Savior. We need to undergo the process of sanctification and be born again from our old life. I was born again as a child, and then as a young adult, I allowed the world's influence to take me away. But I re-dedicated my life back to Christ in the summer of 2000. I was thirty years old. I went to church and did all the things required of me. I served in the ministry and loved what I did with the children there, but I was still broken.

You see it all the time in the church. People singing, preaching, teaching, prophesying, healing, and working in their gifts. People can be successful at what they do but are miserable wretches on the inside trying to cover the misery with the giftings. In every walk of life, as a child of God, using your gifts and not being in the presence of the Gift does you no good. Everything we do, everything I do must be done to give Him glory, honor, and praise. I'm not bashing anyone here, please understand. I am only saying that we must face our lives as they are. We must submit ourselves – ALL of ourselves to the Lord. He must be LORD of ALL of us, not just the parts we want to give Him.

All must be done to glorify the Father in heaven. If not, then why do these things? For the pleasure of men? It may work for a while and even fool the less discerning, but eventually it fools no one, and especially one in particular: God. He loves you and I so much that He will not leave you in your performance. He will lead you to your wilderness, and He will let you see what is there. I saw it. I allowed my emotions and the spiritual darkness that I was not delivered from to take me into places that I should not have gone. I thought I was saved and free from things which dishonor the Lord, but I wasn't. I thought because I could prophesy and had the ability to pray I was ok. I wasn't. I acknowledged it to him, and I was ready to change and get everything wrong right. I covered up my truth and was living a religious lie until Christ shined his light into my heart and set me free.

I humbled myself under God. I saw my sin, asked his forgiveness, and began to walk in the light of His Word. I knew the Word of God, but was it alive actively in me? No. It was simply the letter and not activated and walked out by and through his Spirit. Yes, I performed for a long time, but when I saw my wretchedness, I could not turn away from it. He placed in me, in all of those who desire Him, a longing to obey his word. Even in the little things, I began to listen and obey. Not out of a sense of fear and duty, but out of a sense of real repentance and love for him. I did things now out of reverence and a healthy fear. I only want to please God, and THAT made all the difference.

My husband did not know I am called as a prophet. He only knew that I would tell him things and if he followed it, he would see the results of the instructions from the Lord. He knew I would pray and he is very supportive of my walk with God. He does not stand in the way. He helps me with the ministry that I am now being called to. He understands that God has a work which must be done, and he helps me to accomplish it. Finding my voice in my marriage as I navigated through the many changes took courage. I was unsure how to allow myself to be free in my husband's presence. I slowly began to become more open about my relationship with Holy Spirit. I prayed more openly in the Spirit and I began to really live out what God was inwardly working in my heart. He saw that and began to comfort and console me while I traveled through unknown inner places as I was becoming the woman God has created. When my husband didn't understand, he would silently support me and pray for me as well.

As I said before, as I changed, my husband began to change. He began to see me in a different light and he began to respect himself and me more each day. I began to see God do a secret work in his heart and in mine and made us both moldable in His hands. We are growing in grace and giving one another grace and forgiveness as Christ has done for us. I love him and he loves me. How do I know? Because his actions are proving it. I support his decisions and I wholeheartedly stand by him in whatever he desires to achieve. He is loving himself more everyday as he comes to a greater understanding of his worth in God's eyes. We still have much inner work to do, but we have crossed a threshold in our marriage that I know only God could help us to do. Today, we are better, and we are learning. We are his workmanship and He is continually creating in us clean hearts...He is renewing a right spirit within us. Is it a cakewalk? No, but we are willing, and that is something that God needs from me - surrender so He can walk with me daily.

I do want to say a few things about my experience with a married man. It is never right to interfere in a marital relationship no matter what state the marriage is in. I am not saying this from the judgmental point of view that many women take. We tend to say what we would never do and then judge the ones who do while not fully understanding the journey. We can quote the Scriptures about this and talk about the "sister code" all day long. You can look at me with eyes of disdain. It's fine with me. We say and do things to one another and call it *"doing you."* We can talk about one another to the point of staining someone's reputation. We can get on social media behind the guise of our pseudo names and be mean girls under the guise of "Christianity". We can teach and preach the Word of God on Facebook, in Bible study, etc., and be catty and spew innuendos about one another, and that is acceptable, right? But when we cross into this area, we are unmistakably self-righteous in tone and in thought about the woman who is *the slut*.

I hope you understand woman, that any of what we do to one another to bring harm is sin. And we know when we are doing or saying something about another woman by talking or doing something harmful under the guise of "trying to help" is wrong. None of it is right. Including fornicating with another woman's boyfriend, flirting, getting too close to a man at work, or having a work husband, or committing adultery or any of these things we do to gain a man's attention.

I know it is not right - we *ALL know it is not right* - but instead of judging one another, how about showing empathy? Jesus knew the woman who was about to be stoned was an adulteress, but He did not judge her - He forgave her sin and told her to go and sin no more. When He met the Samaritan woman at the well He knew she was living with a man who wasn't her husband, but He didn't judge her. Instead, He blessed her with Himself, and she went away to share the Good News of Christ with others.

What I am saying is before you go around banging your gavel on the judgment seat, be aware that everyone is guilty of something and sometimes, your empathy and your compassion are the right responses instead of anger and hateful words.

You don't know that woman's story. You don't know the "why" behind her actions. You only know that she is with someone's husband - like the Samaritan. For once, be like Jesus and give the woman grace instead of flesh. Shine the light of Christ's love and pray life for her instead of speaking death over her. Have mercy as Jesus did to the woman about to be stoned. But, if you can't and you pick up stones to throw them anyway, remember that one day, Someone is going to judge you for the stones you threw.

I made my cross, and I hung there for many years. I died to that sin and now I am forgiven and free. I wrecked myself before I checked myself. Will you do the same? Let's do better because we know better. Let's do this together.

Lesson # 3 – Mistakes are Opportunities to Learn and Grow

A broken soul doesn't invest in boundaries because the world has crossed them, without mercy. – Shannon L. Adler

When we make mistakes as humans it can be difficult to own up to it. Most of the time we pass it off or project our mistake onto the situation, circumstance, or another person. It is easier to avoid taking ownership of the wrongs we do than to own it and walk out the consequence of the mistake – whatever that may be. I know I did. I tried to justify my mistakes to God with the pain I received throughout the course of my life. I tried to say that I did it because I was hurting from my past and I only wanted someone to love me. When the opportunity presented itself, I took it not caring or thinking of the results of that choice. We are pleasure seekers. Our nature – the flesh wants satisfaction and nothing else will do. We are living in a society where we want it and we want it now! But God doesn't operate that way. As a child of God, neither should we. The Bible clearly tells us in Romans 6 that we cannot keep taking the gift of grace and continue in sin. If we are in Christ, we have died to sin and that old life is nailed to the cross with Him. All have sinned – all have fallen short, that is why Christ came for us. We will sin as we are going through the life-long process of sanctification, but I truly believe that until we are dead to the old ways and even those things in our hearts that we think we would never do – sin will continue to rear its head to show us ourselves.

What I love about God is that He has provided us through Christ and the help of the Holy Spirit a way to escape the sin which rises to tempt us. Romans 12 says if we fix our attention on God while offering our everyday lives to Him and embracing the gift of Christ as our Savior and Lord, God will bring out the best in us and develop us and mature us. It happens as we are daily renewing our minds with His Word and spending time daily in His presence.

There will always be opportunities to sin presented, but more than that – the opportunity to know God and His Word is there too. We simply have to choose! Temptations will come to try you and will expose what is in your heart, but thanks be to God who will cause us to triumph through it as we submit our lives to Him and not to the sin – we will learn and grow thereby: I know I have.

~ 6 ~

STUPID IS AS STUPID DOES

" Life is like a box of chocolates, you never know what you're gonna get"
- Forrest Gump

I've done some stupid things in my life. I've said things which I thought came out stupid as well. We all have in one way or another done something we regret. In the movie Forrest Gump, Forrest makes a statement that has stayed with me since viewing the film. He said, *"Stupid is as stupid does."* The Urban Dictionary defines this quote saying, "It means that an intelligent person who does stupid things is still stupid. You are what you do, and I totally agree. I lived this out for so many years in my relationships with men, and I'm sharing with you how very stupid I was. In my poem in chapter four, I went through the relationships of my past. I want to go through these relationships to share how bad decision-making was a result of the trauma and sin within me.

After my divorce to my first husband and my decision to stop allowing him access to my body, I remained single and celibate for many years. My children were still little and I could not and would not bring other men around them. I was in the church - religiously saved, Holy Ghost filled, not fire baptized, I was in a state of trauma and it was enough that I had been in a bad marriage. I didn't want to traumatize my little ones any more than they were, and besides

I still didn't know what I wanted. I poured my life into the church, doing anything and everything I could to be a blessing to my leaders and the youth ministry I was in charge of. I became a youth pastor several years after my divorce and I took that seriously. I knew I had to maintain myself for the sake of the kids who were always with me. They had sleepovers at my house with my children and practically lived there during the summers, and I loved it. I wanted to model a life that was pure and holy in front of my kids and all the kids before the Lord because that was what I believed and was taught. As in the previous chapter, I did not know then I was serving men and not God but bear with me.

The church I became a part of was the place where I learned religion. Now let me preface this by saying, I loved my church and the people there. It was not anyone's fault that I learned what I did. It was a mixture of Spirit and doctrine and there was a part of me that yearned for more. I was young in Christ still and was trying to please people thinking I was pleasing the Lord. I gained approval from some through works and not relationship. Don't mistake what I am saying here: I know that works are a necessary part of faith in action, but my motivation for the work was towards pleasing men and not purely for the Lord. It was good works, not God works, and that was a huge difference in how I viewed my relationship with God. He wanted more from me. He wanted a relationship from a pure heart. He wanted me to seek him and not what he could do through me, and I knew that intellectually, yet not spiritually. I looked to my leaders for direction and validation.

I was in a place where others recognized the gifts and talents God had given me, and allowed me the space to use some of them. I held the skewed viewpoint that by doing all these things for people and the church meant I was actually pleasing God. This was not the case. My heart's motivation was misguided, and He, the Holy Spirit, had to show me that.

I was stupid in definition: meaning I was ignorant and carnal to many things in Christ and my eyes were not enlightened to the truth of God's Word. I saw his Word as rules to live by and follow, and I did so in a carnal manner, a works. I was not yet transformed. My eyes were still darkened and my mind still in the old way of "doing." I had not yet learned how to simply "be." I was a new creation in Christ, but in my unrenewed mind, the old things had not died and the new had not come due to my understanding still being in darkness. I believed that I was born-again because I could clearly hear the voice of God, but I have an enemy who used a counterfeit voice and my carnality to entice me.

Lusts of my Flesh

I had much to learn and many things to grow up into Christ, so I believe God allowed my experiences for my growth and learning. One of the things he was stripping from me was lust. I went through years of relationship stuff, so I could learn that Christ is all in all. I had to learn that I had lusts in my heart and I had to learn that it was worthless to go after that and not yearn for and seek after Christ. I was not lusting for sex as much as I was seeking love.

I was lonely - so very lonely - and didn't know why I couldn't shake that feeling of lust that would come over me at the weirdest times. I tried to keep myself in prayer and fasting often to subdue my flesh, but that didn't always work. People can say that it was a demonic influence, and I know that some of it was. But some of it wasn't. It was me in my flesh - my unrenewed self that wanted to be touched. As a child, I negatively learned through the molestations that if I was not touched in a sexual manner, I was not loved. I thought if I used my body to create passion, then I was loved.

The enemy used what happened to me as a tool to keep me in darkness. As a child, the only touch I received was from men, and it was the wrong kind. I didn't get affections from the women in my family. They were not the affectionate type. I love touch, and I love to touch my children with hugs and kisses on the cheek. I tried to give them what I did not get as a child. I was about to be delivered from skewed lust in a major way and I didn't even know it.

My v-jay-jay was screaming and wanted relief! I prayed and prayed and sought the Lord to take this feeling in my body away from me, and I directed that energy into exercise.

Mistake number 1. I would take long walks and exercise constantly to keep myself from going crazy and to stay in shape. I had not learned that my attention was on my body parts and not on knowing Him. It did my physical body some good, but not my spirit.

I did not know why I had so many yearnings for a relationship with a man. I used the excuse that I wanted someone to have companionship with outside of my "sisters" in Christ and my co-workers and girlfriends. What I thought I really wanted was to be with someone intimately. You want to know how very darkened my understanding was? I didn't know what real intimacy was, that I can have intimacy in Christ in the way of closeness and communion. I sought physical sex because I mistakenly identified it as a sick sort of love. I didn't even know that my idea of sex was skewed due to the abuse I suffered as a child.

I didn't know real love or real closeness with anyone because I couldn't really get close to anyone. Closeness was a foreign act towards me. It wasn't something I was used to indulging in with my family. I was close in friendship with my best friend, but that closeness was in sharing our lives with one another and in that even, I didn't. We didn't share everything.

Sex to me was allowing a man to get pleasure while I "took it." I would at times get pleasure from self-manipulation while engaging in intercourse, but for the most part, I let it happen, and if my ex-husband thought it was good, then I thought I did the right thing. I could only receive pleasure from that type of manual stimulation, and I thought that it was the right way to have sexual intimacy. Most of my experiences with my ex-husband were from pornographic movies we watched together. If I did what the women in those movies did, then I thought I was doing something. It made him excited to be with me when I performed some stupid act. When I just did the normal things which most couples do - missionary, etc., he seemed bored or simply wanting to fulfill himself - never mind my pleasure. I don't blame him completely. We were both very young and trying to keep the marriage working. I felt that if I did these things, he would not cheat on me. Yet he already broken our marriage when he brought those images of other women into our home and bedroom. I didn't know how to please men sexually because there was no true experience outside of him. Whatever made him happy, I tried to do to keep him in my bed alone. He cheated anyway. I thought it was my fault, but really it was an issue within both of us.

I needed to be delivered from an unclean spirit, and I had not dealt with the pain from my childhood experiences. I felt as though I was never good enough. I felt the best when, after sex, he went to sleep spooning me. Then I felt intimate with him because he was only hugging my body and not manipulating it to have pleasure. This type of non-sexual intimacy is what I wanted. I wanted to feel something again and not feel empty. My emptiness was not filled with a man's pleasuring himself or trying to please me - it was in my relationship with Christ.

The only time I felt true intimacy - true closeness to anyone - was in my moments of prayer with the Lord. I could literally sense His presence and could get lost in that heaviness in the room. It was as if someone was wrapping me up in a cloak and securing me inside of it. I felt enclosed and extremely peaceful and happy. I felt that nothing in life was better than moments like those.

The Lord was letting me feel His presence so that I can know what real love feels like. He was allowing me the space to lay out in his presence and just be me, without constraint. I could say and be exactly as I was without feeling condemned or having to perform. I could be truthful, and that is what I wanted most - simply to be in the truth. He taught me about himself through prayer and being enlightened by the Holy Spirit as I spent so much time in his Word. He taught me that He is ever present at all times. He knows everything there is to know about me and that He still loves and accepts me.

He feels that way about you too. There is such a comfort to know that there is absolutely nothing I can ever do, outside of completely denouncing him, that would turn him from me. I may have turned from him, but he never turned from me. Yet I still did not realize my truth as a woman created by God.

Our Creator created women according to his plan, which you will find in the beginning chapters of the Bible. In essence, He created us for a greater purpose than we actually would ever imagine. I have so much to share that He revealed and is yet revealing to me through his Word. Yet I had to learn it through my experiences. I became attracted to online Christian dating sites. I was not a paid member of any site, but I did use Christian Mingle, Christian Cafe, and the popular eHarmony sites when they were free. *It was a disaster!*

I was so naive to think that the men I met on these sites were really Christian men who wanted a relationship and friendship that may lead to marriage. I met several men and had several conversations via chat or via email. I didn't feel comfortable giving my number to any of them because I was not sure what the motive was. I met so many men who were not who they said they were, and so many of them wanted nothing but sex and I was looking for marriage. Being lonely will make you do things that you might not have done otherwise - or so I thought. That was my excuse as I searched this website for a good-looking man to become friends with. I knew I wanted to be married, and I knew that I wanted to have someone in my life that I could talk to more than anything. Thinking back on it always makes me laugh at the pure sadness of it all.

The first guy I met was a preacher from a Baptist background who was looking for an educated woman who could sing. I spoke with him a few times, but he did not really interest me. I really wanted to give him an opportunity to possibly form a friendship, but he said one day that he wanted his wife to be an educated woman with an advanced degree, and she needed to be a singer and a homemaker - so I let that one go quickly.

There was another guy, who wouldn't show his face. He only wanted to talk via email, so he was a no go. Then there were the guys who only wanted to be on these websites for a quick sexual experience and that was not what I wanted.

I ended a relationship with someone who I had met on a site who, after dating and investing many months into the relationship, asked my mother and son for my hand in marriage, then turned around, dumped me, and was married two years later to someone else. This relationship lasted over a year. To be fair to him, though, I must say, he was a gentle person who was not sure what he wanted. He thought I was sent to bring him through that dark period in his life. Perhaps I was, but it didn't feel that way to me at the time.

Then I met "Joe." He seemed like a very nice man. We spoke on the phone for several weeks and even planned to meet. He lived in the NE part of the country. All of a sudden, I stopped hearing from Joe. I called and his phone went to voicemail. Then one day, I get a collect call from the jail. The Jail!!! Joe was arrested. I won't go into the details as to why, but he told me he would be released soon.

So stupid me, I never thought that I would waste my time with this sort of situation, but I did. I researched his arrest and found out he was released. He did eventually write to me and basically told me when he was released he needed a "little time" to himself. He then commenced to tell me that his daughter told him I was a weirdo, and that he shouldn't connect with me! I was the weirdo? He was the one who went to jail and then wanted to have a "little Joe time"! This was a few months long. I was scammed for two years by an African man who stole from me - my money, other people's money, and my emotions. He would say in his thick accent, *"If you do leave me, I - will - shot myself"!!!* Yes, that is how he said those words. I was so hurt, in some ways, I wished he had. Sounds cruel?

Yes, but that is how I felt at the time. I did have the pleasure to let him know how I felt about his deeds, but I was angrier with myself for allowing this to go on for so long. This is a true indication that I did not love myself and I was so needy!

Needless to say, I stopped trying to meet men in any capacity after that. A few months went by and I attended a church meeting and met a feisty preacher. Well, I didn't meet him officially at that time, but there was an attraction. We developed a friendship over the course of several years after I emailed him and we spoke about our feelings. I began to invest a lot of time, emails, and some money into this man. Not that he asked me to do any of it. In fact, he would often ghost me until he wanted to talk.

This man thought I had a Messiah Complex, and when he would visit the church I attended to preach at the revival, he would ignore me in front of the other leaders, yet he would call me at night at random times to talk. I thought I was in love with him, but he was not interested in me.

This back and forth continued sporadically for three years. He wouldn't say he *was not* interested and what I thought about him was wrong. He told me he didn't know. I believed in my heart that he was the person for me and had confirmation from others who did not know that we were even secretly communicating. This continued until I got tired of hurting and moved on. I heard later that he married from the Bishop's announcement when he returned to preach another revival. You won't believe this, but he and I reconnected after many years. He is doing well. Divorced, with a beautiful son and is now a Bishop presiding over his own church. We had a long conversation about what happened in the past, and he sincerely apologized. Back then, he was very ambitious, and had a plan for himself that did not include me. He told me in essence, I was too settled and he wasn't ready to settle down. I certainly can understand that now. We are friends, and I'm glad about it.

It's amazing how good can come out of so much turmoil. I was too desperate back then for someone to love and God knew that. I went through every relationship to teach me about my own lack of wholeness. After all these men and six years of my time, I still could not see that I was not healed enough to have the right man approach me. I was like the woman in the garden who was told not to touch the tree or the fruit. However, I fell into the words whispered to me, and I was naive and broken. I touched the place I shouldn't have when I was not ready and received the consequences of my insecurities and undisciplined life. Yes, I received one hundred-fold the pain from my own relationships. I felt as though every blow to my heart was earned. One thing I know, is that God can take every miss, every trial, and every hurt and make it good. He can turn my ash into beauty and my muck and mire into a river of life. But I had to learn and learn I did.

Lesson #4 - Epiphanies

What did I take away from this chapter of my life? Even when you have the best intentions in mind, the road to hell is paved with those good intentions. Hell (Hades) is overflowing with people who had good intentions, but heaven is overflowing with people who do God-works; even when your good deeds are evil spoken of. Do what is right and you will not go wrong in God's eyes. What was my good in this case? It was simple: I wanted my life to be better, and I wanted to have it with someone who accepted me for me, yet how I reached for those things was totally incorrect.

I was like the parable about the seed and the sower where some fell in weeds and the weeds choked the word. That was me. I was strangled by weeds of rejection and hurts from past relationships so much in my heart that although I received the Word of God, it was strangled by all the darkness still within me.

Matthew 13:22 says: *The seed cast in the weeds is the person who hears the kingdom news, but weeds of worry and illusions about getting more and wanting everything under the sun strangle what was heard, and nothing comes of it* (MSG)

I was not ready for a relationship because I did not know who I was or what was best for me. I was untilled soil, and bad seed was planted in me which produced a tumultuous harvest. All the Scripture I studied went out of the window, and I succumbed to my desires. The lust of my flesh, the lust of my eye, and the sadness of my life produced a pride in me that made me selfish and desirous of external things.

I was Nola Darling from the movie *"She's Gotta Have It,"* and I did. I took it and reaped a harvest of heartache. Yet in becoming a version of Nola, I, like she, came to the truth of me. My truth showed me who I really was, and it set me free. It is freeing to finally know that you can take the pressure off of yourself and face you. It is freeing to see that although I am a wretch and the worst of all, I am still loved and accepted anyway. That allows me the space to see myself, accept myself, and love myself as I am, because Christ does.

If you are a single woman and are considering having a relationship, make sure that you are ready. Ask yourself, "How can I know that I am ready?" Check your soil. What is in the innermost part of you? Have you come to a place of loving you? Are you emotionally, physically, and spiritually secure where you can say that you are whole and completely you? Are you bringing your confident self-loved whole being to the table in the relationship? Where are you within?

If you can answer that with a resounding truth and authenticity - I'm not saying answer yes but answer with truth - then perhaps you are ready to accept seed in your soil. Know your soil and know the seed you are going to accept into your soil as well. It is equally important.

If you are a single man, consider this: maybe the dog in you has not been mastered. Devon Franklin, notable author, preacher, and producer wrote in his book: *The Truth About Men,*

> *Lust is an overwhelming selfish impulse for sexual,*

> financial, professional, or personal fulfillment by any
> means necessary, even if those means are personal,
> professionally, or spiritually detrimental...I call
> this lust the Dog. Every man has lust, aka the Dog,
> within, and when we allow that lust to go untrained,
> unmanaged, and unmastered, it can cause men to
> behave just like an untrained dog. When fed, this
> Dog can become powerful enough to destroy every
> good thing men have planned for their lives.

Pastor Franklin's book used the term dog to describe the behavior of men who have not mastered and balanced their lives. It is descriptive of the sometimes-overwhelming desire to dominate things, people, etc. I brought this into my book to say to men that whatsoever seed you distribute will yield that type of harvest. If you are still out there and living an undisciplined life - you are not ready. If you don't have the woman's best interest in your heart - you are not ready. If you are struggling with addictions of any kind - you are not ready until you can face you and deal with you. Until you come into your truth, you are not ready to have a really authentic relationship with a woman.

For women, the term bitch according to Merriam-Webster is descriptive of a female dog. It is also informal and often an offensive word to mean a malicious, spiteful, or overbearing woman. A woman who is not in step in her truth and has difficulty dealing with past emotional scars can be malicious, spiteful, and overbearing when she and her desires are out of balance. A woman cannot blame it on PMS - although it can affect behavior at times. Both terms describe people out of balance and in need of God's loving truth applied and living in their hearts. The end never justifies the means in the case of overriding one's morality to fulfill the desires of the moment. To master this area and live in authentic truth results in a higher living and maturity which extends beyond the self towards others. It takes the consuming fire of God to cleanse the heart, and the overwhelming power of the Holy Spirit to counsel, direct, and keep you.

Lesson # 5 - Relationship Lessons of a Christian Woman's Life

Number 1: If you are still hoping one day you will get married and focus mostly on that and not on the Lord's will and preparation for marriage by becoming a whole you, you are probably not ready.

Number 2: The heart wants what it wants, I heard someone say in a movie and its true. If your heart is panting after what it wants more than what God wants for you - you will not hear Him speaking or will ignore His unction and will miss His direction.

Number 3: Don't shake upon another person's tree to get their fruit. Hurting someone else to fulfill your needs is going to backfire on you. You can cross into someone else's yard and steal their fruit, Eve, but the consequences of that action will result in your pain and will cause a rippled wave effect that you may not be able to swim out of.

Number 4: Remember to watch what and whose seed you are receiving. We are receivers by nature. We were born to receive seed. If a man comes into your life and is bringing you his seed - watch the type of seed to see if it matches your fertile ground (assuming you have done the work of preparing your garden and your soil is fertile and ready). A seed in bad soil will harvest corrupt fruit, but seed in good soil will yield a harvest of goodness. What type of seeds are you receiving in your soil? What type of soil do you have to receive seed? Is your soil ready?

Number 5: Sir, don't be a *dog*, and woman don't be a *bitch* - discover who you really were made to be - who you really are, and your self-indulgent titles will change and so will your life. It did for me.

~ 7 ~

WAITING TO BEGIN...AGAIN

"Declaring the end from the beginning, and from ancient times the things that are not yet done, saying, My counsel shall stand, and I will do all my pleasure:" - Isaiah 46:10 KJV
And God said, "Let there be Light, and there was Light" - Genesis 1:3 KJV

I am out of the proverbial people closet!!! Hallelujah! I am free of people's opinions, people's acceptance, people norms that I simply do not fit in. None of us are "norms" - we are all different. We are beautifully unique patterns in a galaxy of patterns all genetically balanced to blend - not to conform. How did I get here? It was not an easy path to travel, nor a pleasant journey to take.

I've always been different. You know what I mean? That one person who does not necessarily fit in anywhere. That's me. What was an embarrassment before is now my banner which I wear proudly? I *LOVE* being me. I hated being everything else, and I lived in that world for more than forty years. I wanted to be true and live in my truth. I wanted to grow and evolve into the woman I knew was inside of me. I wanted to really live out my life without apology and without hiding. I wanted to laugh instead of crying, cheer myself on instead of feeling shriveled up like I was dying. I felt like I died inside. I felt like I had no life if there was no real me.

For years, I would look in the mirror and see images that didn't look like the "inside" me. Ladies, can you relate? That "you" no one sees but you. That "you" that no one appreciates but you. My inner "she" was raging to come out of the proverbial closet, but I couldn't really be the woman I knew that I was. I was still hiding.

I hid in my home with my spouse. He wanted a certain type of woman, and I became her in some ways. I hid on the job, because I had to dress a certain way and act a certain way. I had to wear my hair in a way that was acceptable to the majority - even though it was clear that I was not a part of that majority based on the color of my skin. My skin tone, and the way I carry myself is intimidating to some. It is not my fault that some ethnicities cannot accept my place as an African American woman in the earth. We are meant to be who we are: regal, spiritual, beautiful, unique, and incredibly intelligent. We offer much, yet sometimes receive so little, unless we take it. Horrible in this day and age, right? I mean, goodness, in the twenty first century I still have to conform to the majority rule when I was never a part of the majority. That seems a bit ridiculous when I think about it.

Now, before you start saying I have a rage or anger, let me clarify I am not angry. What I am though is over the fact that in order to get a smile or acceptance from you, I have to dumb down me. I have to conform to your imagination and stifle my creative bloom. I have to be for you what makes you comfortable, and all the while I am uncomfortably walking around in my skin, just to make life better for you.

I certainly do appreciate the strides that people have taken to wake up and understand the truth about the human race; that we all bleed the same color blood and originate from the same Eternal Source, but we are diverse and should be free to live out our diversity with full acceptance and love. I know...sounds like nirvana and will not happen in my lifetime, but I do recognize the strides being made to make our world a place where we can live and just be great! Not great again, but simply great. How can we be great again when all of us are not doing great? I'm not bashing anyone, but if we're going to embrace the slogans, we have to embrace all that comes with it right? I proudly wear the slogan *free Nisei'* because *I am free!*

I rest in my freedom from opinionated people who are probably miserable and want the lives of those around them to be more miserable than theirs. I felt sad that I bowed to misery, and I felt sad that I allowed misery to take up company with me for so long. I pray for those who maliciously troll social media to be mean little girls and boys on another person's page. They don't understand that they are hiding too. Hiding behind their mean words because they themselves are hurting, sad, angry, and mad about whatever monster is chasing them. So, how do you become true and live your life out loud?

There is a famous quote by Shakespeare, *"To thine own self, be true,"* which has been spoken by many people throughout the ages; but how many of us today are *really true* to our own selves? I cannot begin to try to answer that question for you: nor do I wish to. I do wish to convey something in my heart concerning the true self which is still baffling to me. Why can't we not only be true, but *stay true* to ourselves? Tuning into the self requires that a person complete an inner self check to see what's going on. What this does is connects us to our own body, mind, and soul and tunes us into our "higher selves."

What psychology deems as the higher self, I say, refers to the conscious within. People are so busy with many things today. Our lives are filled to capacity with activities, events, work, kids, issues, and brain-overload - so much so, that who can hear through all the outer noise and the chatter which continually rings outside and within the mind? Tuning in takes so much courage and bravery. Why? Because tuning in shows a person what's really going on inside. Whatever truth one knows and/or learns about oneself is good. It is what we actively do about what we know that will either change us forever or will continue the perpetual merry-go-round of the phases I described above. This type of being can only lead to a very shallow existence.

So, I looked in the mirror one day and thought, *Why can't you just love you?* I did not know how. We could have better lives, marriages, relationships, work experiences, and churches if we only come to and walk out the truth given to each one of us in the self; yet so many of us continue in the messiness of deception. It seems we are comfortable in not knowing. Although I have not heard every negative connotation someone ever said to me or about me, I knew I had to come out of that thinking.

I then begin to pray and meditate on why I was hiding. Fear caused my hiding. I was afraid that I would be rejected, afraid that I would not be accepted, afraid that if I was really myself, I would not be good enough or liked enough or loved enough. I had to learn that fear and truth could be the vehicles to move me into the best life or fear alone could paralyze me to stay the same. I decided to let fear drive me. I took a long walk on the inside and got my stuff together, and now I am free! My freedom also came from the strong realization that God, in His Infinite wisdom has planned out every part of my life. The parts where I failed, He used to shape me. The parts where I walked in fear, He used to show me Himself. The parts where I obeyed Him, He used to process me and cause me to be more like the image of His Dear Son, Christ. In all things, His love for me watched over me - carefully He used every part of my existence to bring me to where I am now.

How am I being free you ask? One word now comes to mind and that word is *Emerge!* The Webster's dictionary says to emerge is *to become manifest: become known. To rise from: come out into view. To rise from an obscure or inferior position*, and my favorite definition is *to come into being through evolution!* I began to look inside myself. It was hard to cut down the inner noise and look within. After I began to take a look at what was going on the inside, I began to see a pattern. This pattern was a wave that kept me spiraling back and forth and tossed to and fro rooted in fear. I was afraid also to be disappointed again. I was afraid to recognize the talent and gifts that I was given by God to use for his glory. I was taught in church that you cannot be too high-minded about your gifts and talents. You had to be 'trained' on how and when to use your gifts, and it was usually when leaders said you were ready. In the walls of the church, you could not step out and just be used by God. This brought fear. When I was a child, I was told to go and sit down because again, I could not simply be myself - whatever and whoever that was at the time. It was as if I was always being stifled by someone. I was always being told I was not ready. I felt inferior and very, very small.

The Church

In the church, the Lord would sometimes give me revelatory information for the local body of believers or for a particular person. I would have to ask permission to speak to that person from the leadership, and if I was told to hold the message and not say anything, then I would. I did not understand at that time. It was God who gave me the message in the first place. I knew that God called me to the office of the prophet and used me in the prophetic. I was being taught by the Lord how and when to use the revelatory gifts. I was not offended by being told not to say anything, I just did not understand because as I read and understood the prophets of the Scriptures, they did not need permission from anyone but the Lord, because the spirit of the prophet is subject to the prophet (1 Corinthians 14:32 KJV). This means literally that prophets are subject to one another.

I also know that we are co-laborers with God in Christ and we are to be respectful of one another and subject to those who lead us. This should not be abused, and everyone should walk in love and service to one another. I do believe and understand why leaders in the church would try the "spirits" to see if it was of God, because they felt a tremendous responsibility to the people to ensure they would not be harmed by those who would come in and speak false words to the congregation. At times, speakers would come to preach and they could miss it. We understood that this can happen and to "eat the meat and spit out the bones." This means take the truth only and discard the rest. I still struggled with it all. It was an inner struggle where I battled in my mind against the negative words injected into my head about church leaders authority.

The enemy's battle ground is the minds of people. If he can get you to think it is you speaking to yourself, or if he can counterfeit the voice of the Holy Spirit, it can be difficult to know which way to turn. I spent much time in prayer and reading the Word of God to have the discernment of who was speaking to me. It takes time and if one is not careful, the enemy can still deceive the mind of saints of God. We must be filled with the Spirit of God in fullness. We have to stay ascended in Christ, so we, the elect, are not fooled. I was immature in the faith, but what I did know was that I knew the voice of the Holy Spirit, when He was unctioning me to say something. I was told that God does not speak to a person as much as He was speaking to me, but He was, and I knew it. He would tell me things that would happen before they came to pass. I would just watch it happen in front of me just as He said it would. I believe it was my training ground. He was training me to know Him and to recognize His voice.

In church, I was used as the leaders saw fit for me to be used. I was allowed to teach, speak at women's conferences, and to lead in the children's ministry. I was allowed to be a part of the worship ministry, and several church committees, but in prophecy, I was restrained.

I get it now. There were more seasoned prophets in the house, and also I was looked upon and titled as an evangelist, then youth pastor. I was not seasoned yet, and at times when the Holy Spirit gave me a word, I was too afraid to speak. His Presence was unfamiliar and I was still learning, so when He would rise in me very strong, I would at times become emotional and the delivery was not skilled and honed in. I was not trained in exercising the fruit of temperance (self-control), and I could not hold back the emotions from feeling His presence. Over time though, He has trained me to be calm and quiet when needed, and strong and emotional when needed. I have learned to allow Him to have complete control. I do this by letting go and letting Holy Spirit take control of my mouth to speak. He has full use of my body to do whatever is needed. I humble myself in my heart before Him and ask him to have control. I give up my own way and thoughts and give myself over to His will. It is all by faith that I do these things, and His training me over the last 21 years.

Back then, my fear of letting loose in the house of God was inwardly terrifying. So many times, I wouldn't say anything when the pastor would ask if anyone had a "word" because I feared my emotions would make me look bad in front of everyone. I feared men more than I feared God, and that was not good. The gifts of God are without repentance, meaning God does not change what He has already given. So, he would use the gift more outside of the church walls where He knew people would listen. I know because my eyes were on people and not on God, I did not see that it was His Spirit within me preparing and moving me, I could not see that He was giving me balance. My focus was off, but the gift was not.

I shut down because of the words of people. I was once asked by a few of the women if they could join me at my house for prayer. I immediately said yes because I wanted community, and I desired sisterhood and friendship. We began praying on Saturday mornings at 5:00 AM at my house and would switch to another woman's home frequently. In those times of prayer with these women, the Lord moved in such tremendous ways. Women were being set free and delivered from issues right there in my living room. The Lord was providing us answers, and we had an awesome time as we gathered together to fellowship and worship the Lord. I'm not sure how it happened, but we were then told by the leadership to stop having prayer in our homes, and we were to come to the church to pray. I told the ladies it was their choice if they did not want to continue coming. Some stopped, and then God sent others. It was amazing to see that I was not advertising prayer, the ladies were led to me, and the Lord told me to obey Him, and I did. As I obeyed, the Lord Himself did great things with us. This is where I saw trouble beginning. My heart was broken because of the opposition I begin to experience with some of the women. The youth ministry to which I was called was thriving. The Lord was blessing us because our hearts was right before Him. I did not want accolades, what I wanted was for my leaders to recognize my heart for service, and to validate the call of God on my life as a prophet, yet, It was not time. God was still processing me.

I could not understand where the jealousy was coming from. I only wanted to be saved and to serve, and it seemed that my desires were being scrutinized and criticized. I was called upon to speak in other ministries, and I went, but I was hurting the entire time. I didn't have the support of some of the most important people in my life, and I somehow attributed it to not pleasing God. I searched my heart and I fasted and prayed, but the Lord kept directing me to continue doing what I was doing in spending time with Him.

One evening, a friend who is a prophet called me and said He had a rhema word from the Lord and came by to tell me. I was anxious because I had not spoken to anyone about my pain, only the Lord. He came by and simply told me everything I had been praying, and what God said was shocking. He would call me forth from that ministry if the leadership did not acknowledge His call on my life. I didn't want that, but I knew it was true. I did not want to hurt them – although I was hurting, but I knew I had to obey the Lord. The prophet left my home and I sought the Lord again concerning His will.

This happened over a three year period. The Lord then said for me to step down from all my duties and seek His face alone. I received so much backlash from that decision, but I prepared for the time when I would step down. I made curriculum guides for those who would take my place; I also made a guide for the Worship dance team and appointed someone I knew could take the team forward. I left the ministry after this and after a few months of seeking the Lord I was directed to attend a church we were connected to.

The Lord sent me there but I did not want to go. I knew I was not wanted there, and the congregation knew I would be there a short time. What was that for? To teach me that my eyes must be on the Lord. I allowed my emotional state to rule me and my decisions instead of trusting that God would show me the way in His timing. He still used the gift outside of the walls of the church, but it took a long time for me to realize that I needed emotional healing in order for the true balance in prophetic ministry to emerge. It is true that hurt people hurt others, and church folks inflict the deepest wounds. I was deeply wounded by those who I cared for and loved, yet I now know it was all for good. I can go on and on, but I am doing this so that you will understand how we can truly wound one another by our own thoughts and lack the leading of the Holy Spirit. This is not a "calling out session," but I want you to be aware that God's love does no harm. When we walk in His love, we see from His perspective. 1 Corinthians 13:1-7 says:

> *If I speak with human eloquence and angelic ecstasy but don't love, I'm nothing but the creaking of a rusty gate. If I speak God's Word with power, revealing all his mysteries and making everything plain as day, and if I have faith that says to a mountain, "Jump," and it jumps, but I don't love, I'm nothing. If I give everything I own to the poor and even go to the stake to be burned as a martyr, but I don't love, I've gotten nowhere. So, no matter what I say, what I believe, and what I do, I'm bankrupt without love. (AMP)*

What does God's love do? It cares for others more than self, isn't about me first, doesn't fly off the handle or keep score of someone sins. Love isn't glad when others fall. Love looks for the best and puts up with anything. I was not experiencing this love, and God was allowing me to see that. I took the pain of those experiences and went with Lord into the wilderness so He could teach me more about Himself. He taught me love, for He is love. This is when He told me to go and I left organized church. One day He said to me *"Go where I say go, say what I say, and do what I say do."* This has been His directive to me and this is how I follow Him on a daily basis.

Let me say this: I do not blame anyone in the churches for anything at all – in fact, I am thankful. We are all the Bride of Christ, and even as leaders, we are often the ones who are hurt by those we lead. Sometimes we unknowingly hurt those we lead as well. It is important for leaders and lay members to experience healing and develop in spiritual maturity so they in turn may bring healing and hope to others according to the Spirit of God and His guidance. As Paul said in 2 Corinthians 1:4:

> *What a wonderful God we have—he is the*
> *Father of our Lord Jesus Christ, the source*
> *of every mercy, and the one who so wonderfully*
> *comforts and strengthens us in our hardships*
> *and trials. And why does he do this? So that*
> *when others are troubled, needing our sympathy*
> *and encouragement, we can pass on to them*
> *this same help and comfort God has given us.* (MSG)

We must bring our hurts as leaders to Christ for healing so we in turn can allow Christ to heal others through us. Paul aptly tells us our responsibility to one another as *We are only God's coworkers. You are God's garden, not ours; you are God's building, not ours* (1 Corinthians

3:9 TLB). We have to be mindful that we are working together with God to bring salvation to the lost, and healing to those who need it. I believe that my experience at that season of my life was to teach me to trust in God and to lean on him completely. Yes, we need one another, for that is why Christ died for his bride, the church - but the lack of acceptance in some places leads to discouragement and often times, people experience hurt from being manipulated and controlled by those who are walking in the flesh and not the Spirit of God.

So, I left organized church, and off I went with the Holy Spirit who led me into a wilderness in order to teach me his ways. He led me away from religion to show me the truth about me and the truth about God. What did He show me? He let me see that I still had a lot of sin in me. I made decisions emotionally which led to testing my character, and I found it to be severely flawed. Things I never thought in my religious self I would do, I found myself doing. Things I thought I would never say in my self-righteousness, I found myself saying. It was the small foxes that were spoiling the anointing in my life, and He had to cleanse me from all unrighteousness in order to use me the way I was made to be truly used. One thing I know for sure, is that the truth about me hurt to see and acknowledge, but it was that same truth with God's inner work and His word which made me free.

The Sexual Self and My Essence

One of the things I acknowledged was to understand my whole self. Including my sexual self. This part of me was the sole reason why I was in so much trouble with men. It was why I had issues in my relationship development with God. It was why I had issues submitting to authority because men represent authority in the earth. It was why I had issues in my sex life in my marriage. It was why I had so much emotional turmoil. My dad's death left me without an example of proper authority - an example of how to understand my femaleness - my sexual self. The molestation of the men in my life took away the beauty and innocence of my essence. A father becomes in his daughter's life the example from which she follows. A dad represents to his daughter the idea of wholeness through his connection to her. He is the alpha-male and what he does carries the most weight in her eyes. She looks to her dad for validation, and she seeks from him the ways in which she can be taught about love. She watches his interactions with her mother and learns so much from his perspective so that she can have both mom and dad's view on life, love, dating, and boundaries. Dads are a symbol of God as Father. Leading as protector and strength provides her the safety needed to feel she can make good choices. She can grow in the fullness of her being through the example of both parents, and as an adult, become a woman in her full essence: She is complete and beautiful.

What is a woman's essence? It is in a nutshell – her inner beauty showing on the outside. It is more than her physical appearance. A woman's essence shines when she is in the fullness of herself: mind, body, and spirit. She knows who she is and she knows she is worthy of love. She loves herself fully. She understands her sex – female disposition – is speaking. She is beauty, she nourishes, she comforts, she helps, she transcends, she draws. This is essence. I did not receive from my dad what I needed to become this whole sexual being as a woman. In speaking in terms of being sexual, I am referring to every part of my female sexual being. It was taken at the age of five.

Childhood sexual abuse perverted my understanding of my womanhood - my sexual essence. Molestation tainted my view of the male, and since God is seen as male in position, it tainted my view of Him. I didn't know who I was because I did not have the example, and I experienced sexual traumas which took away the innocence, pleasure, and beauty of hetersexual love. Understanding who you are as a sexual being is a very important part of relationships, and marriage in particular. It is a part of identifying with who you are as a person.

Some people who have experienced sexual traumas have issues with their sexual selves as adults. It has a lot to do with how you perceive yourself, and your view of how others perceive you. My self-perception of sexuality as a woman was something I needed to deal with. I had not in the past dealt with this area. It was untouchable – partly because I thought what I was doing was correct and partly because I didn't want to deal with it. I was okay with settling for whatever happened in the bedroom because I thought if he was happy that is all that matters. I have found in speaking with many other women, that this type of behavior is not uncommon in marriage. But it is not okay. Some men believe sex is a performance, and if they don't think you are satisfied, then that messes with their ego. In order to make my ex-husband happy, I would fake sexual pleasure to the point that I really was fooling myself to believe that what I was experiencing was all there is to it.

But it was in my second marriage that I came to the revelation of the truth. God revealed this to me and I felt so undone. The Lord kept speaking this scripture to me, *"Physician heal thyself"*(Luke 4:23 KJV). I know that there is a larger connotation to this Scripture, but when spoken to me, it was Him saying that I have the tools within me for my own healing. Going through things and fully understanding the why of it all helps me to heal. I found this to be true shortly after this revelation in my heart.

I was able to speak to my husband about my heart, and how I did not know how to fully engage in sexual love. He was very surprised, and we had a very hard conversation, but he is so understanding and loving. We took a season of discovery together. It was work, but pleasurable work. I finally understood sexual love, and I was so content. Yet I was not happy with my body and was very ashamed of how it stretched out from babies and weight gain. My husband never complained and he actually complimented me constantly and is very affectionate. I was not satisfied. I wanted to look outwardly how I felt inwardly.

I had cosmetic surgery to correct some issues I was having. It changed my life completely when it came to my physical self. I understand and embrace others who are comfortable in whatever way you are comfortable. I am expressing this about me. I was tired of hiding my body from my husband during intimate moments. I wanted to feel beautiful and I was not feeling that way. I desired to have an abdominoplasty (tummy tuck) for many years. I prayed about it, and the Lord led me to the right surgeon and coordinator at the right time. I was at peace with my decision, and so I went for it. It was one of the best decisions I was led to make. Yet I still had issues. I loved my physical body but did not like the attention I was receiving from others. I didn't like the stares of dislike from other women who did not know me but judged me on my body shape, and I certainly did not like the stares from men ogling me as I passed by.

The Lord let me see that I had comparison issues, and that is when the healing in this area began. I no longer wanted to feel like I had to make an excuse or apologize for wanting the surgery, having the surgery, or loving the way I looked post-surgery. I wanted to be free from the feelings of self-degradation, from hiding under bigger clothes to not draw attention to myself. Freedom and understanding your essence as a woman has a lot to do with how you see yourself sexually. Sexuality was given to us for procreation and for pleasure (see Song of Songs 1:1 and Genesis 1:22). One thing I do know is that Christ wanted me healed in every area, and that included healing from sexual sin. I know that once I asked Jesus to forgive me for my sins; that his death and resurrection cleansed me, but I had to walk that out in my life, and I was not yet doing that.

In my case, healing from sexual sin meant those committed against me and those I committed. I did not go to therapy for this. He brought healing to my heart though the truth. My self-perceptions affected my encounters with my new husband, and this behavior was very telling. My husband is a wonderful human being, but he could not give me the answers to my healing, nor can I bring answers to him, but Christ can. When healed, I then began to understand who I am as a sexual being. Not my sexual preference, but my whole sexual self as a person of the female sex. Because some do not understand their sexual selves, there has been an insertion of perverseness into our lives.

Our sexuality in a lot of ways becomes skewed because of the way things have been infiltrated into our minds. Unless you have been living anywhere else on earth that does not have social media influence or another human being, you know what I am talking about here. Perverse does not mean bad, it means crookedness. A way of thinking that is not straight is perverse. So not that you or I are terrible perverts...we have been introduced to crooked things and as a result have experienced perverseness and allow it in our families because it has become a way of life. In Scripture we are told to turn away from perverseness (Philippians 2:15 KJV). As a child of God, I want to live my life as a beacon of light, not in darkness and crooked stubbornness. I know that some will read this section and say that my whole life was crooked, and you are partially right. That is what is so sweet about having a relationship with Christ. He makes all the crooked places – the perverse places - straight.

Sexual health is important, and especially in our community, the community of women around the world, for we have been ravaged by sexuality in some form or another. Perverseness which invaded our space has distorted how we understand and view ourselves. To each woman, your preference is your own; I'm not getting into that. I am merely speaking about understanding who we are as sexual beings.

Because some of us do not understand (I didn't), our sexuality, our sexual essence has been skewed by the worldviews we have adopted. According to an article on the essence of sexuality, gender roles have been argued by many in the feminist and scientific world debate of nature vs nurture causality. However, author Diana

Richardson defines essence as this: *"Your essence is what actually animates you so that if you are out of touch with your essence then you are basically pretending to be someone that you have never been."*

This article is speaking specifically about heterosexual relationships. The article also said that masculine essence follows the feminine, so, if a woman is out of touch with her true essence, a man won't fare so well in his interactions with her. There needs to be a sort of separation of essence - for if a woman is like the man in demeanor and interaction, there is no attraction. Getting back to knowing your self is to know your true essence.

To become reconnected with your essence is to connect with your truth. When a woman connects with her whole self though healing her femininity, she then understands she is an added attraction. It comes out through her being, and her confidence, and is reflected in her outward physicality. Look at the biblical woman in the Song of Solomon. She was a rare beauty indeed, and her essence is what spoke volumes to the writer, who is depicted as King Solomon. This type of sexual essence exudes from a woman in a way that is naturally and spiritually attractive. It will attract anyone. When a woman knows her essence, it attracts things to her. All things which were created for her purpose and destiny are deep within her. This Shunamite woman in the Song of Solomon had a beauty in her voice. Her voice to her lover was of confident elegance. She knew she wasn't always beautiful to others, but she refused to allow it to dim her light. Her essence flowered from her at the right time. She said, "When my King-Lover lay down beside me, my fragrance filled the room. His head resting between my breasts— the head of my lover was a sachet of sweet myrrh. My beloved is a bouquet of wildflowers picked just for me from the fields of En Gedi" (Song of Solomon 1:12-14 MSG).

As she walks in an essence that is nourished correctly and whole, her purpose and destiny begins to come up and out of her. She begins to see her truth and will confidently walk out her journey from the inside out. She will flourish. An essence which is perverse attracts the wrong things and people to a woman. This is a sub-attraction. It was what was going on inside of me. I had perversion from childhood which affected my relationships as an adult. This childhood perversion attack wielded a seed and that seed grew into a root of lust and perversion. This false essence is what I lived from. It attracted the wrong seeds to my garden and I grew nothing but weeds.

An essence that is healed and a woman who truly understands who she is at her core will attract unto her the right people and things. I needed that healing. I wanted to become that woman whose essence was pure and who understands her sex, her femaleness, which is a gift from God.

I wanted to become purely attractive instead of things being subtracted from me because I did not know my female gift of essence. Because my essence was perversely learned there was a lot of subtractions in my life; but when I was healed at my core - and my essence, my inner soul has been purified, then good things were attracted to my life. It will be attracted to you specifically made for you and for me. Why? It is coming from your essence - your core. Your values, your sexual self, your wholeness, your real self - must come from the core of you and that is where God is working in us. As we seek him in this area, He will add to us or show us what was already added to us since the beginning of time. *"Seek first the Kingdom of God and His righteousness and all these things shall be added unto you"* (Matthew 6:33 KJV)

God has a right way of doing things, and because he made us to do what is right from our core, he will show us the way back to added pleasures. He is working from the core of each one of us as we allow him and acknowledge to him that we need his help. When you look at biblical Eve at the beginning, she came out from the man. She was a part of him. He actually was subtracted from (by the taking of his rib) and then God added her into the earth. So, she was always an addition. Never was she built to be a subtraction. She was built to be an addition.

When she came into the earth via the part of the man God took, she added back to him what God took, and plus some. Why? God added to her everything that was missing from him. He gave the woman everything that was missing from the man. This is why the Word says that *"It is not good that the man should be alone; I will make him a help meet for him"* (Genesis 2:18 MSG). God took the addition of the woman and brought her to the man. He attracted them to one another. She was specifically for him. This is a law established by God as He made them and recognized them in the earth. Her essence is an added attraction. She is necessary to not only add to the man with her physical self, but she is to add to him through helping him in everything he needs. She is complete already. It was the enemy's job to make her think she was not complete and that she needed to have something else. She compared herself to what the serpent told her, not understanding she was built with everything she needed for God's glory.

My worldview on female sexuality had me bound up by a standard which was very unrealistic. I entered the world of cosmetic surgery shocked at how many young and older women were getting the surgery to look 'snatched' because of other "dolls" *(is what they are called)* looked like. I didn't want to be a doll, I wanted to be the best version of myself physically. Not for my husband, even though he was receiving the benefits from my surgery, but for me. There are also many women like myself who want to be their best physical version, but my view was still skewed concerning how I should look even after my surgery. There is a scripture which enters my heart and it says, *"Oh, don't worry, I wouldn't dare say that I am as wonderful as these other men who tell you how good they are! Their trouble is that they are only comparing themselves with each other and measuring themselves against their own little ideas. What stupidity!"* (2 Corinthians 10:12 TLB)

It is foolish to compare yourself with anyone, yet that is one of the big things God was showing me concerning my sexuality that was really foolish. I could not help myself though. My inner insecurities were a major part of comparison. I was constantly comparing how I spoke, and how I looked compared to other women in that Facebook surgery group, although I knew that at my age, my healing would be different and perhaps slower anyway. I still looked at those women with their perfectly rounded butts and flat stomachs and wondered, *"Why am I not shaped that way?"* Although I knew in my mind and from research and education about cosmetic surgery, that each body type and results would differ, I still kept comparing. I was not shaped that way because I was not them! I was shaped like me, and I had to learn to accept me - and that was my problem.

I compared everything all the time: What I accomplished in my life at my age with others my age, how I couldn't finish this book while others have written three or four books to my one unfinished one. How I raised my children compared to other parents I knew. The lists of comparisons went on and on. In this country comparison is a major thing with our young people on social media. Western society - clothing chains, social media stories, etc. - has taught our girls and younger women that showing off something or going and having surgeries for the praise of men is sexy. The songs which literally tell young girls how a boy wants to be 'done' sexually is from a crooked place. Even female songs speak of a woman's body parts enticingly, and they let a man know what they want from him without shame. Some women have become a feminine version of a dirty old man who yells out at a woman as she walks down the street, and it's become our norm. According to that aforementioned article, it is not attractive. I'm not bashing how these young men and women feel about their bodies or their music, but I am concerned about the message it sends to our young girls.

It is a skewed worldview, even to the point now that some parents allow their daughters to utilize this perverseness on social media and say, *"That is cute,"* and even participate in it. I know that many will say I am wrong for saying this and there is no harm in dressing provocatively, and dancing and shaking what your momma gave you. If that is what you want to do, then it's your choice.

What I am asking is, what if you just stop and ask yourself *"Why am I doing what I am doing?"* It would show you things about you that maybe you had not seen before. It would perhaps give you pause, and perhaps deter your decision-making based on societal norms or emotional necessity.

We cannot control how others perceive us, and I am certainly not judging you because I shake it every now and then too; I love to dance. I also have social media accounts and like to have fun with them. What I am saying is this: Have we allowed our thoughts about our bodies to become what is believed to be so free that we give it out to the world with no thought about it? I totally get that many women over 40 are rediscovering themselves, and are becoming freer with their presentation, but as Christ-filled women, what is the motivation for your actions on social media? Is it for likes on Instagram, Tik Tok or Snapchat? Does it matter who likes the snippets of your filtered self?

I am not asking anyone to stop being who you are but think about it...before Tik Tok and these other social media outlets, we were in the church shouting and praising and dancing before the Lord (post salvation). Now we are doing the dances on social media and what true purpose is it going to serve? Trust me, back in the day I danced in the club like there was no tomorrow, and especially to reggae music! I was winding it up and didn't care about anything and anyone, so I definitely understand. Adults understand dancing this type of dance is a form of sexual freedom and expression; it's an outlet. It is enticement.

Is that the message I want to send and encourage our younger girls to display? I believe that there is a time for displaying your shake...and an appropriate age and place to display it as well. If we listen to God, if we follow his precepts, and have a relationship with Him, He will show us the real truth about why He created sexuality and embedded it into our essence.

God's Word states that we should have an abundant life that Christ died for even as we are abundant from our essence: our soul.

It's a soul healing needed. It was what I so desperately needed and obtained. I am only sharing this with you because of the major impact it has had on me. I'm not bashing anyone. I am asking you to think about the "why" behind what we allow to happen on our social media accounts. You are not responsible for another person's perverseness, but you are responsible to protect yourself. I am careful as well with what I post because there are wicked spiritual forces out in the atmosphere who wait and relish in any opportunity we give to make Christians diminish. We are cities on the hill. Beacons of light which shine in the darkness. We have to remain lit - if you will - in order for the world to see Christ, our hope of glory in us. This includes our children. The Bible teaches us to *Train up a child in the way he should go [teaching him to seek God's wisdom and will for his abilities and talents], Even when he is old he will not depart from it* (Proverbs 22:6 MSG)

As we teach our young people the ways and precepts of the Lord while being a good example, and exercising parental boundaries, we give them the opportunity for growth and freedom to be children as we protect them from the darkness which is trying to invade our homes, our cellphones, and our smart technology devices.

I just want you to think about it. That is all I ask. I encourage you now to close this chapter and just think about what I said. Then write down your motivations for what you do for you and for those who are attracted to you...including your children and close relationships. I know that if you really take a moment and think about it, you might see a need for change.

There are so many books out here that can show you the steps to gain joy, or how to walk in peace, etc....but this book is messy, and it's not all prettied up and put together because my life was not that way. Someone needs to understand her essence and learn from my mess. A very wise man of God said to me that the crushing of my life has caused me to operate at a lower level to where God wants me to be. He said that when I realize what God has done in me, I will rise with Him and that rising will bring me the confident humility to walk out who I am - without shame. I am now walking in that higher narrow kingdom, and I am ready to attract everything God has for my life - His way and in His timing.

~ 8 ~

IT'S NEVER TOO LATE

"It's never too late for a new beginning in your life" - Joyce Meyer

As I'm sitting here and wondering what the heck I think I am doing thinking that I could actually write a successful book, I feel like an imposter. I've felt like that for a long time, until I heard a talk which First Lady Michelle Obama took part in, and she spoke of Imposter Syndrome. Her words struck a chord in my heart as she said, *The question of "Am I good enough?" has stalked me most of my life. How I overcame that is how I overcome anything...Hard work. Whenever I doubted myself I put my head down and said, Let me do the work and let the work speak for itself.*

This was an amazing epiphany I received from her. It resonated so deeply within the core of me. I know it unlocked a reservoir of renewed strength and an openness to receive and to achieve my God-given purpose. I wanted to work and let my work speak. That imposter syndrome had to die.

Imposter Syndrome is defined as doubting one's abilities and having feelings as if you are a fraud. This is what I felt like for so long when I was attempting to write this book. I tried to do it in a way that I felt society would accept. I wrote what I thought people wanted to read about. Being a Christian, I thought I had to write about how God can deliver you, keep you, save you and lead you on this thing called a journey through life. I tried to write things that I thought people would say were deep, dope, relatable, prolific, prophetic, revelatory. I wanted my book to have humor, to show that I am not always serious. I wanted it to be serious to show that I am not a silly woman. I wanted it to be intelligent to show that my education did not go to waste. I wanted my book to show that I am an awesome individual that people want to get to know. I wanted to show my good side...but instead, I have pages and pages of the mess of me.

I am not those things all the time, but does that really matter? Sometimes I'm sad, and sometimes in my life I regret the decisions I have made. Sometimes, I want to express the sheer struggle to actually get up out of my bed. I want to express my pain, but who wants to read about that? Everyone has pain. So, I write about the injustice of being black in a world where being a woman of color is still an issue with others. I write about the frustrations and the joys of my marriages – both of them. I write about the things I did in both my marriages that I wish I could erase and do again. I wanted a *do better - not a do over* and I wanted to share it.

I sit here with tears on the inside of me just screaming to get out. Tears from so much...of everything, of my life. I share my joys... my real joy. I write about the shame without fear of judgment. I put my poetry in here. Not the great poctic words of Maya Angelou (my shero), but my words...my peace, my pain, my sorrow, my anger, anguish, hurts, healing. I tell you how I really feel. I am authentically transparent, but really what does that look like? It's everything I just said and more. It is me, plain and simple. Me and myself, my soul, my spirit. So maybe this book won't reach anyone that I think it will, but maybe it will reach those who need it. And, if I can just stop trying so hard and just say what is in my heart, it will flow. It will grow into something beautiful, if not for you – then maybe this overflow inside me is healing waters for me. Maybe it will answer someone's questions. Hopefully my truth can save someone from going down the roads that I have traveled alone. But even if it doesn't, even if my words are rejected like I have been rejected, I will still have shared my life with you. I will have walked in my season where I know that God has led. He led me to write. He led me to say what I saw, encountered, went through, learned and am still learning. So, because I know he leads me, I write.

Because I know he told me to write the book and he would do the rest, I write. Because I know that in writing, I am being helped, instructed, regenerated, rediscovered, I write. I know that in the spiritual and natural realms, the changing of seasons means something new is coming. And now, I am the moth that has struggled to emerge from my chrysalis; I am emerging into what? My unique season of rebirth into the real me. My colors in my wings unlike any other. My flight strong from the fight within, I now emerge into my season. I cried today. I cried as I emerged. It was cleansing and invigorating at the same time. I cried today. For the time I put into people and felt so not appreciated in return, yet I know I am loved. I cried today. Because in all the mistakes I made, God has turned my life around for good. I needed Him to hear this cry. I needed Him to hear this prayer...this one prayer I prayed from my inner being today.

In my heart I heard God speak to me and say a scripture. I went to my Bible and read it. It was Ezekiel 37, and He said to my heart:

> *"Behold, I say unto you, that you will live.*
> *Your dry days are now over, and you will live.*
> *Not only will you live but you will prophesy to*
> *others who are in dry places to come forth.*
> *When you speak to them, I will thunder and*
> *rattle them and they shall shake and quake and*
> *come alive. I will fill them with My Spirit, and*
> *they shall hear My voice. They shall know that*
> *I Am God and I will be their God and they shall*
> *be My people. With a fervor and renewed fire shall*
> *they go forth and serve Me and I will be with*

them wherever they go. Your complete life as
you know it, the dry places of your life shall now
be watered. You shall go forth with wings as an eagle.
You shall run and not be weary and you shall walk and not faint
- Prophetic word based on Ezekiel 37:5-6,
and Isaiah 40:31

So, I know that this is my season. It is time to say what is in my heart and to do exactly what God has said. So, I prophesy to you that if you have been dry, if you have felt like you are dead on the inside, and if you feel like God is not there - I prophesy to you to LIVE! God IS THERE! He wants you to acknowledge Him, and He will thunder on your behalf and you shall come alive! Ask Him and He will fill you with His Holy Spirit! He will speak and you will learn and come to know His voice! I pray you receive through my words comfort, answers, and hope. You can come out of your shame. You can have the life God purposed and planned for you. I am not ashamed anymore. The Holy Spirit has turned my ashes into something beautiful, and for that I am grateful. And so, I write, and so it is. I have Emerged and so shall you!

Amen.

~ 9 ~

IT ONLY TAKES FAITH

And he said unto them, why are ye so fearful? how is it that ye have no faith? (Mark 4:40 KJV)

And Jesus answering saith unto them, Have faith in God. For verily I say unto you, That whosoever shall say unto this mountain, Be thou removed, and be thou cast into the sea; and shall not doubt in his heart, but shall believe that those things which he saith shall come to pass; he shall have whatsoever he saith. Therefore, I say unto you, what things soever ye desire, when ye pray, believe that ye receive them, and ye shall have them. (Mark 11:22-24 KJV)

It is not too late for me. Nor is it too late for you. In the past, I felt as if my time was up. I am a middle-aged woman who has so many dreams that have yet to come to fruition. I have served another man's dream for so long, and I did it without complaint. I served in ministry, and I did it without complaint. I have a career which I enjoy which serves my community, and I do it without complaint. Yet deep inside, there is a dream so big it is beyond my scope of natural thinking.

It began to spring up when I emerged and the Lord opened my eyes to see a need in my community. As I sought the Lord about it and asked his help for the sake of this community, He began to reveal to me what and how this need can be met. It is a huge undertaking, and one I know for sure will take the Lord's direct hand to get it accomplished.

I have shared this dream with others in my inner circle and, for the most part have been supported. But It wasn't their dream, it was mine. Although those I trusted to keep me accountable and on track didn't have the faith as I did for this undertaking, I had to stop talking about it, and simply pray and asked God to confirm His word to my heart. Any endeavor you find inside that is bigger than you and not for you, I have found it is usually God seed. Yet the bigger the task, the more I was tested. Doubt was sown into my mind the minute I took my eyes off God and placed it upon people. I have found that it was not for them to have faith for what God gave me – it was for me to have faith and to speak what God says over this dream and obey His will concerning it.

This seed He has revealed to me for the past eight years has been growing on the inside. Have you ever felt that there was something really BIG you had to do, but you didn't have a clue as to how it would be done? I still am not quite sure how the Lord will accomplish this, but it is not for me to know, it is for me to believe. Faith comes by hearing the Word of God. God spoke His Word to me, and I have confirmation on his Word in Scripture. I then must take this and apply it to my belief system and wait for God's instruction.

As I wait, I worship him, and continue to walk in love and to serve as I know how to do until He shows me my next steps. I know I am in direct alignment when I hear His instructions and I move step by step into His purpose. This whole waiting while you worship thing was and is sometimes very hard for me. I am a doer. I love to make plans and get things done.

My flesh wanted me to believe I was wasting away time when asking God about things, and then waiting on the next instruction. I believe these were the times when my faith – my belief system was and still is being tested. Once in prayer, I asked the Lord to show me what was wrong. He said that I was like Martha, busy doing things, but not understanding the most important thing which is to simply be with Him. I have Martha tendencies like nobody's business, and I have to catch myself sometimes from getting involved in good works before consulting the Holy Spirit first.

I used to ask Him everything before, and then I thought I didn't have to do that as I followed Him from the inside. I became lazy and stopped consulting Him before rushing ahead to get myself involved in another project of some sort. It was when I saw that my own life was going nowhere, that I decided to stop and seek Him again. Then He began to reveal to me that I was not flourishing, I was simply surviving Christianity. I still had so many issues in my heart about faith and believing God for myself that I was setting up my own way of walking with God when really I was walking on without Him. He was with me, but I was not with Him on anything pertaining to me.

I needed to go back to the Word of God and begin to allow His words to teach me in the way that I should go. He took me to the parable of the sower in the book of Matthew. I went over and over that portion of scripture until it was revealed to me what I needed. I need the Word of God planted in the right soil of my heart. Throughout Scripture God shows us how to grow in grace and from faith to faith and glory to glory. It is through the development, pruning, and planting of His Word in our hearts that we grow thereby. I had developed a hunger for His Word at one point in my walk with Him, and then I let the cares of this world pull me away. I became distracted with the world and how it wanted me to work, instead of looking at God and how He wanted me to *be*! It is such a revelation to be made humble and whole at the same time. It is a process and one that I am sure I will continue to go through on this journey. The Lord wanted me to see my heart as soil and His Word as the seeds. He was creating in me a renewed sense of purpose and transforming my mind. This mind which I speak of is not only the conscious thought processes but the deeper mind of my heart – my inner person. So, He began to take me on a journey into the garden of my heart.

Seeds take time to grow after being planted. I remember as a young girl in elementary school, one of my teachers brought in seeds for different flowers. She was teaching us how plants grew. She used clear plastic drinking cups and filled them with beautiful, nutritious soil. The soil smelled so good to me as I placed my soil in my cup. She let us gently pour drops of water in the cup to dampen the soil just a bit. Then she gave each of us two seeds. I placed my seeds in the damp soil and lightly covered them over. She had us place them in the windowsill for sunlight, and we placed a stick in our cups with our names on them. It was our responsibility to check our cups and make sure the soil was wet and our cups were getting sun. That was all we had to do.

I watched over my cup diligently and was excited to see some green poking through the soil one afternoon after lunch. It didn't take long, but every day I watched over that cup like it was my baby. That's how I needed to be over this seed the (Word of God) planted in my heart. I must watch over it and keep it watered by speaking it. I must let the Son shine in my heart so the seed can take root and grow.

My mom used to talk to her plants. She said they loved it and would respond by standing up straight and tall when she spoke to them. She was diligent over her houseplants, and they were absolutely beautiful! The leaves were lush and green, and the flowers, if they were flowering plants bloomed so brightly.

I needed to use my mom's method spiritually with my seed. I had to be diligent over my seed by speaking what God's Word said about my life. I had to water my seed daily with prayer and study of the Scriptures. I had to fertilize my seed with faith and watch it grow over time. I was not doing that at first. It was quite an eyeopener to see my lack of belief concerning what God said. I had many people speak words over my life which never came to pass.

My eyes was on the words and not on the God of the Word. I was emotionally drained and spiritually dried up. My heart was the soil in the thorns. I received the Word, but then when trials and hardships came, I became tossed and walked in disbelief, and the Word was choked in my heart. The Holy Spirit cannot move unless God's Word is spoken in faith. I was speaking but not believing. I said it in my mind, but it was not in my heart, nor was I saying it out of my mouth. I needed a heart transformation, and the Lord took me through what I call the five stages of building my faith.

Stage 1: The Revelation of the Dream: The Sprouting of Faith.

The seed is revealed. This is when the dream or vision or purpose is revealed to you. It is something that you have not thought of before. It is something beyond your natural reach and it is for others and not necessarily for you. Although you will be blessed from it, this dream or purpose extends out from you to meet a need or solve a problem. At this time, I was really excited that this thing could happen and I would finally be walking out my purpose in a major way to help others. In this stage, you also make the dream, vision, or plan plain by writing it out, making a visual presentation, or by speaking to others about it. You may even begin to research more into how you can make plans of action to get things done.

This is the beginning of your faith for this vision or dream to happen. I not only wrote out the dream, I prayed and asked God to show me what to do. He led me to the facility and it has everything needed to bring this vision to pass. I love teaching vision board classes and enjoy teaching others about faith and believing for their own dreams to manifest. I made myself a vision board of the vision God planted in me, and I hung it where I can see it the most: in my office. This was my way of seeing it before I attained it. It was my sprout in the ground. I found several Scriptures that I was led to in the Bible and printed them out and placed them on my board as well. This Scripture was the base scripture for my seed: *For the* faith mixed with God's Word is like the watering of a sprout *(Hebrews 4:2)*. I didn't want to be like those who hear the Word of God and do not mix it with faith. I had to keep his words to me in my view to stay aware of my vision. Now let's look at this in the natural.

If you plant or garden, there is a process that the seed goes through in order to become that plant which bears fruit. The first stage is the seed sprouting stage. The seed contains every nutrient it needs to germinate and grow the first leaves. This is like my vision. God shared his desire with me and planted it in my heart. Everything I need for this vision seed to bear fruit is *already* in the seed. I had to acknowledge this and believe that God had placed this vision in me and wanted to use me as the soil to bring it to fruition.

In the natural, when a dry seed is planted, the seed absorbs the water, and this is called *imbibition*. Imbibition causes the seed to swell with maximum force. The seed then breaks open, and the important radicle forms into the primary root. The Holy Spirit in my spirit is the maximum force the seed in me needs to force it to open and begin to root itself into the core of me. For the Scripture says, He that believeth on me, as the scripture hath said, out of his **belly shall flow** rivers of living water *(John 7:38 KJV)*.

Stage 2: Aeration - Activation of Faith:

There is a requirement in activating my faith that I was not aware of. I needed the breath of the Lord to breathe on the soil of my heart in order that I might give my seed aeration. What is aeration in plants? It is the introduction of air into a material. When air is applied to the soil, it makes the roots grow into healthier plants. What is my method of aeration? Speaking the Word of God over my seed. Opening my mouth and giving breath to the vision allows my vision - the dream to breathe as well. In the beginning of the world, God spoke and said, *Let there be light" (Genesis 1:3).* He spoke, and it was so. The Holy Spirit - the breath and wind of God moved and brought the spoken words of God to life. God spoke and it was so, and He has given us that same ability when He created us in his image and likeness.

We have what He has because He is within us. The great I AM lives in us by His Spirit. Our voice is what we need as we speak forth the word of life over the seed. It does not matter that you cannot physically see it. In the beginning, there was darkness, and then God spoke for light to appear. God didn't see the physical light - He spoke and it was done. God breathed in the darkness, and his breath made his spoken word come to life. We must in turn look past the things we do not see and breathe on the vision - the seed - and say 'let there be light'!

In the natural germination process, the watering of the seed causes metabolic activity in the rehydrated seed, and respiration of that seed begins. Energy provided through what is known as glycolysis causes aerobic activity as oxygen enters the seed. Seeds of aquatic plants germinate under water by using dissolved oxygen. But seeds planted in soil receive their oxygen from the air within the soil. Although most seeds are sown in loose soil near the surface topsoil, planters plow and hoe the soil to give it aeration which encourages germination.

We in turn, must plow through the darkness - the negative Nancy's, the Nay Sayers, the spiritual wickedness that will try to plague you with doubt and fear, through those who don't believe. Even God when he spoke to bring forth light didn't pay attention to the darkness. He didn't acknowledge it nor take heed to it. He spoke his desire, and it was so! Give breath to the vision by speaking it! Using the tool of the Word of faith and the power of the Holy Spirit who is the breath of life. Say what He says, and keep saying it, until you see the light of that vision shining brightly through. That is faith in action!

Stage 3: Respiration – Illumination of God's Word Feeds Faith

Another requirement in activating my faith was that I needed the light of God's word to respirate through illumination in my heart so that I could believe. Faith is made through my hope that what is promised to me will come to pass. How can I have faith without the illuminated word of God within me? The Scriptures read that the Word was made flesh – Christ – and the Word is a lamp unto my feet and a light unto my path. The Word of God lights the way of hope so that my faith can stand and begin to grow in my heart, thereby increasing my belief and continuously feeding my faith to believe God for the unseen and the impossible.

In this stage of seed germination, respiration or light upon the seed allows the seed to take shape in response to the light. Some seeds grow best in positive sunlight, some seeds grow in negative light – darkness or night light, and non-photogenic seeds germinate in light or darkness. As the seed absorbs the light needed, it begins to transform light into metabolic energy. All germination at this point is dependent upon the quality of the light to which it is exposed. As you continue to expose the light of God's Word in your heart in any and all seasons, dark seasons, gray seasons, or light seasons, your faith will continue to grow.

Stage 4: Dormancy- The Waiting of Timing in Faith

When a seed is viable or alive and ready to grow into a flourishing plant, there are times when it does not germinate right away. This is called dormancy. This state – even in optimal conditions keeps the seed from experiencing bad weather spurts or from being eaten by herbivores. It is a cunning way to keep the seed alive while it is waiting to sprout out of the ground. When walking by faith, there is a Scripture that stays with me when I am in the waiting stage of my faith to bring the promise to pass. Isaiah 40:28 – 31 says:

> *Don't you yet understand? Don't you know by*

> *now that the everlasting God, the Creator of the farthest parts of the earth, never grows faint or weary? No one can fathom the depths of his understanding. He gives power to the tired and worn out, and strength to the weak. Even the youths shall be exhausted, and the young men will all give up. But they that wait upon the Lord shall renew their strength. They shall mount up with wings like eagles; they shall run and not be weary; they shall walk and not faint.*

While I am waiting on the promise of God, I am still loving and doing good towards others, but there are times when I grow weary and my faith is tested. These are the times when it looks as though nothing is going to happen. With a natural seed, this means that there is a hard-thick coating on the seed which needs to be cracked open. It can be broken by soaking the seed or scarifying it (scratching the surface until there is a break). My seed faith is soaked as I continue to speak His Word over the promise and I continue to walk as though it is happening although I have yet to see it with my eyes. I have to remain in faith, like Abraham did and the countless others who waited for the promise with their eyes on heaven, knowing that even if they didn't see it here on earth, God will still keep His word, and in that they can be comforted. God never grows tired - even when I do. He renews my strength and gets me to the place where I can continue and mount up in faith and wait. For I know that one day, I will see the seed pop up from the ground and begin to grow. I will see the fruit of the promise as I watch, water, and wait on him.

Stage 5: Breakthrough and Birth of Seed

With a natural seed, it will begin to rupture, the root grows into the ground and begins to take in the nutrients and minerals. Then the leaves of the shoot break through the ground. The seeds divide and break forth into little plants. I am entering the season of breakthrough and birthing of the seed. In my family, there has been breakthrough and blessing. There has been times of good things happening that has not happened before. But now is the season where the breaking in my life is producing the birthing of my promise.

Your time of breakthrough will come as you wait on the Lord in faith and be of good courage. The Lord knows the exact timing of your breakthrough and He knows when you will be ready to produce fruit. John 15:1-8 says:

"I am the Real Vine and my Father is the Farmer. He cuts off every branch of me that doesn't bear grapes. And every branch that is grape-bearing he prunes back so it will bear even more. You are already pruned back by the message I have spoken. "Live in me. Make your home in me just as I do in you. In the same way that a branch can't bear grapes by itself but only by being joined to the vine, you can't bear fruit unless you are joined with me. "I am the Vine, you are the branches. When you're joined with me and I with you, the relation intimate and organic, the harvest is sure to be abundant. Separated, you can't produce a thing. Anyone who separates from me is deadwood, gathered up and thrown on the bonfire. But if you make yourselves at home with me and my words are at home in you, you can be sure that whatever you ask will be listened to and acted upon. This is how my Father shows who he is—when you produce grapes, when you mature as my disciples" (MSG).

Everyone in Christ will undergo this faith journey. The Father loves us enough to take us through it time and time again as we walk with Him. We must remain joined to the Lord, and allow Him to plant the seeds in our hearts. We must water the seed with faith, and worship, and when the time is perfect, and you are perfected enough to carry the weight and responsibility of the vision or purpose God has for you to accomplish - it will surely happen! Don't separate yourself when the season of dormancy comes. Just keep worshipping and wait. Don't drop the vision because the time seems long, remember He knows the exact timing for your vision to come to pass. He said so and so it will be.

~ 10 ~

THE REIGNING SEASON

"Endings are not always bad. Most times they're just beginnings in disguise"~ Kim Harrison

This book is my seed in the earth and the birth of this book is the beginning of the promise coming to pass. As I continue to believe in God and in His Word, as I continue my walk with Him knowing He is God and He loves me, I will prosper. I shine because He is light and He is within me. I'm in my reigning season because He has overtaken my life and is reigning in me. God has launched me out into the deep places of His will and it is expedient that I keep my eyes on Him. I have learned, I am not alone, but God is with me in ALL the things of my life. He was with me as a child and He watched over His word concerning my life. The devil had a plan, but God's purpose is far greater than any wiles of the enemy. God has His hand upon my life and it is evident.

He was with me when I fell, He was with me when He picked me up and cleansed me from unrighteousness. He was with me through ever hard place, every trial, every triumph, and every dry place. He never let me down, and He Himself taught me the way I should take as I follow Him by His Holy Spirit.

God caused me to grow in the wilderness of my soul and I am now flourishing. Psalm 92:14 says, *they shall still bring forth fruit in old age; they shall be fat and flourishing* (KJV). These are my latter days, and I am producing fruit. There was a song which was sung by a very sweet and dear woman to my heart. She sang it specifically to me at a time when I was at a very low point. The words which took root in my heart helped me to hang on when I felt I couldn't. These words are now coming to pass in my life:

> "The winds of change are blowing
> What is now will be no more
> Due season is now come upon us
> This is what we've been praying for
> The windows of Heaven are now open wide
> And showers of blessings pour on us like a tide
> It's the latter rain. It's the latter rain
> Oh, it's the latter rain" (Alvin Slaughter)

As I am completing this book, my mother went to be with the Lord. She overcame breast cancer over 20 years ago, however, it was non-small cell lung cancer which overwhelmed her body, and she finally gave up her life. I say she gave up her body because she was ready to leave this earth to be in the presence of Jesus. It's funny how things happen isn't it? The human body is an incredible organ, and it can literally heal itself from an ailment, but the ailment returned in a different form and this time, when it was discovered, she made the decision to stop fighting. I am reminded now of the schemes of the devil. He is like an ailment to the body of believers, and he is sneaky and tricky. The enemy, the devil, comes to steal from us the very life that Christ died for. He enters in one way and brings a feeling of defeat, death, and discouragement. But we are aware of his devices, and we know that we have the ultimate victory over him in Christ Jesus. The battle is not ours; it is the Lord's, and death is swallowed up in victory. Although my mother's body is left here, her spirit belongs to God. "*O death, where is thy sting? Thanks be to God for giving her the final victory!*" (1 Cor. 15:55, 57 MSG).

Even in her pain, she was always encouraging and loving. She told me that I can accomplish anything I set my mind to. My mother was prophetic in her words to me. She came to visit me while I healed from a surgery just 5 months prior to her passing. She was there for me in every way. She was being my mom. She had a way with words, and when she spoke, she did it with clear intention, and her words were full of meaning. She did not mince words with you, and she always spoke of the Lord in anything she admonished anyone to do. My favorite scripture she spoke often to encourage me was Isaiah 64:4, which in essence says that God has things prepared for us that we have never seen nor heard before. As I listened to her when she spoke that scripture to me, I could sense she was seeing things from Heaven's point of view, and I felt her words as if they were coming from the Holy Spirit. I knew that she had my back in prayer, and that one day, her prayers for me would come to pass.

Her final words to me before she stopped talking was *"finish the book."* I promised her that I would, and so I have. Most people would say that death of a loved one is a process that is so individual - so personal that unless you walked in that person's shoes, you could not possibly know what it is like. I feel that way about my mother. Losing a parent is a difficult process. I lost my dad at age five and that is how I began this book - with death and now I end it with my mom's death and my newness of life.

The end of my mother's life here on earth is significant to me. It is not happenchance that I am finishing my first book eight days after she transitioned. The number eight in biblical terms means new beginnings. What I know for sure is that there is a new beginning here. It's my rite of passage. God has something BIG up His sleeve and I am privileged to be a part of it. This book is a part of my purpose that God created me for. I love to write, and I intend to make writing a priority now when before it was an afterthought or creative leisure I partook of that brought me peace. I know that my Creator has a plan for me and for you too.

Jesus went through such a process to reign now as Lord and King. He came to this earth to be our example, and everything he went through was for a greater purpose. His birth, journey through his childhood, His ministry as a young adult, and death, burial and resurrection from the cross was for me. It was for us to have the right to be saved from eternal death so we could live eternally with God. He came to save my soul and it cost Him everything. Sometimes, the processes we go through as we journey this life seem so harsh. I listened to an audiobook of a very prominent actor's beginnings and the trauma she experienced, I know, many could not imagine. But, every part of her story exemplified her strength of character, her resilience as she fought through every battle, and her peace as she is now reaping the benefits of coming through her storms.

I too have battle scars. So, do you. I went through every part of my journey, not unscathed, but built to become the woman of God He originally intended me to be. It cost me everything. God knew every trial I would face. He knew my faith would be tested. He knew I would sin and get lost for a season, and He also knew that He would bring me back. I was a sheep led astray by my tragedy, but God in His love and mercy came for me and returned me back to Him. I now understand that my journey was not for the faint of heart. My journey was for me to be humbled, to grow in grace, and to become transformed like a beautiful butterfly. His glorious image and likeness is working in me and for that I am so gratefully glad.

Don't look at my story as a sad, bitter tale of a woman who was lost, but see it as I do: A story of redeemed grace and love from Father God to his daughter. See me as a woman not scorned but torn from a scarred abusive existence to reigning on earth as it is in heaven. See my story as lessons learned, victories won, and faith revived and transformed anew. Although my life did not have the start or the middle that I would have wanted, God trusted me with this life so He can get the glory. He wanted me to tell my story so others can see that He truly does love us and He is surely with us – even when we don't think He is or want Him to be.

When God has a purpose for you, nothing will stop His plan from happening - not even you. He took my messy life and turned it around for good. He made my ashes turn into beauty and He made everything about what I have been through beautiful in its time. He can definitely take your life and do the same. The beauty of this story is that *it is my story* - and it is worth sharing.

My mother's death means that my life must now continue where her physical life ended. She had so many hopes and dreams for her family. She desired most of all that we would love God, serve Him, love each other and others and be of some good in this earth for God's glory. The glory of God was certainly upon her life and this passage of scripture aptly examples this,

If ye be reproached for the name of Christ, happy are ye; for the spirit of glory and of God resteth upon you: on their part he is evil spoken of, but on your part he is glorified (1 Peter 4:14 KJV).

My mother suffered and sacrificed her whole life for family, her siblings, her children, her grandchildren, and her great-grandchildren - so that our lives would be better. O matriarch - you are so honored! What greater glory can she receive than the glory of God resting upon her.

As I continue onward in my journey of life, I will remember that the struggle of over fifteen years to complete this book was well worth it. For in this struggle, I discovered my freedom, I rediscovered myself, I have come through my triumphs, my losses, and defeats. I discovered that God was with me and had His hand upon my life - even when I believed otherwise. I found peace with my God, my family, and my life like I have never had, and a quiet joy from knowing that I completed a promise to my mother that I didn't know could exist. It's the Latter Reign of God showering my life. He is reigning supreme and He is continually transforming my life into something beautiful.

So, to God I say, be glorified and to my mother, I say...thank you.

To you I say, trust God with your journey. Even in the mess, God shows up in His best just for you, to guide you and be with you in all things. Why? Because He can trust you with your journey, your trials, and your victories, and it's all for one reason: for His glory!

May He shower you with love, light, and blessing, and I hope that this book has given you something to think about. Maybe even something to talk about, and definitely something to share.

Until the next one, I want to leave this Scripture with you, for this is the basis of who I have become in Christ, *Then shall we know, if we follow on to know the Lord: his going forth is prepared as the morning; and he shall come unto us as the rain, as the latter and former rain unto the earth (Hosea 6:3 KJV).*

ABOUT THE AUTHOR

Denise Wedington Jones was born and raised in Paterson, New Jersey. Denise considers her faith and family to be most important to her. She is a transformational leader, author, blogger, podcaster, and educator. She has founded Denise Wedington Jones Transformational Life Coaching, LLC., and The Flourishing Life Group, which serves as a safe space for women to grow authentically in Christ Jesus.

Denise's passion and call is to witness the movement of women beyond the barriers of life to flourish in their God-given purpose. She has launched her powerfully impactful Revive & Align Retreats which facilitates workshops, coaching, counseling, and ministry to teach women how to become the women God called them to be in faith, transparency, authenticity, and truth. She believes in the supernatural power of God to transform lives as they walk in faith and victory.

Denise has authored poetry and Bible teachings which includes her latest book, Latter Reign. Her next book, The Alignment Plan will be released in 2023.

www.ingramcontent.com/pod-product-compliance
Lightning Source LLC
Chambersburg PA
CBHW051451290426
44109CB00016B/1707